KS3 ENGLISH IS EASY

(READING – FICTION, PLAYS & POETRY)

www.How2Become.com

As part of this product you have also received
FREE access to online tests that will help you
to pass Key Stage 3 ENGLISH
(Reading – Fiction, Plays & Poetry).

To gain access, simply go to:

www.PsychometricTestsOnline.co.uk

Get more products
for passing any test at:

www.How2Become.com

Orders: Please contact How2Become Ltd, Suite 14, 50 Churchill Square Business Centre, Kings Hill, Kent ME19 4YU.

You can order through Amazon.co.uk under ISBN: 9781911259015, via the website www.How2Become.com or through Gardners.com.

ISBN: 9781911259015

First published in 2016 by How2Become Ltd.

Typeset for How2Become Ltd by Anton Pshinka.

Printed and bound by CPI Group (UK) Ltd, Croydon, CR0 4YY

Disclaimer

Every effort has been made to ensure that the information contained within this guide is accurate at the time of publication. How2Become Ltd is not responsible for anyone failing any part of any selection process as a result of the information contained within this guide. How2Become Ltd and their authors cannot accept any responsibility for any errors or omissions within this guide, however caused. No responsibility for loss or damage occasioned by any person acting, or refraining from action, as a result of the material in this publication can be accepted by How2Become Ltd.

The information within this guide does not represent the views of any third party service or organisation.

CONTENTS

UNDERSTANDING THE CURRICULUM

THE NATIONAL CURRICULUM

State-funded school pupils are taught a curriculum of 'core' subjects. These core subjects teach them skills which are paramount to creating well-rounded and educated citizens.

In Key Stage 3 (ages 11-14), the core subjects that must be taught in schools include the following:

- **English**
- **Maths**
- **Science**
- **Art and Design**
- **Citizenship**
- **Computing**
- **Design and Technology**
- **Languages**
- **Geography**
- **History**
- **Music**
- **Physical Education**

All schools, from Key Stage 1 to Key Stage 4, must also teach Religious Studies to their students; and from the age of 11, children will also be taught Sex Education. However, parents are given the option of pulling out their children from these lessons.

THE IMPORTANCE OF ENGLISH

Students are taught English via spoken language, reading, writing and vocabulary. Not only is this a core subject which all students are required to undertake, but this subject is an integral part of other school subjects. Children will need to have a strong grasp of the English language, and this will prove vital if they are to be successful across their other school subjects.

<u>The fundamental aims of the English subject include:</u>

* Reading with fluency and ease;

* Demonstrating a good understanding of the English language;

* Highlighting the importance of reading, and allowing students to read for both pleasure and academia;

* Learning to appreciate the English language and its heritage;

* Acquiring a strong English vocabulary in order to improve students' ability in reading, writing and listening;

* Practising how to write effective literature, adapting their writing and language with a purpose, context and audience in mind;

* Improving children's confidence in their English abilities, allowing them to become competent in the English language via verbal and written communication.

In Key Stage 3, the English subject focuses on four main 'disciplines':

* **Reading;**
* **Writing;**
* **Grammar and Vocabulary;**
* **Spoken English.**

The aforementioned disciplines are all used in order to teach students vital skills for both academia and the outside world.

READING AND WRITING

Reading and writing form the very basic skills that every person should obtain from an early age.

Reading can be done for pleasure, as well as for learning new information. The ability to read is necessary across other school subjects too, and therefore it is important that students are able to read fluently and effectively.

Writing is another great skill, which can be altered to reflect different contexts, purposes and audiences. In Key Stage 3, students are required to write different literary texts, for different purposes. Thus, this requires a strong level of vocabulary and grammar.

GRAMMAR AND VOCABULARY

Students in Key Stage 3 will need to build upon knowledge which was obtained in Key Stage 2.

Teachers will need to enhance students' knowledge by teaching them the importance of grammar, punctuation and spelling. These key areas allow students to not only analyse literary texts, but also improve their own writing style.

Linguistically, students will need to develop a strong understanding of English terminology, and learn how this can be applied to literary texts. This includes learning how to use appropriate vocabulary and understanding the meaning of words and phrases, as well as learning the ability to analyse, practise, and apply literary techniques to their own work.

SPOKEN ENGLISH

Not only is written communication an important aspect of the English language, but the ability to speak fluent English is just as vital.

Spoken English is used every day, in a range of different contexts. Developing a person's speaking skills will allow for well-rounded citizens who have the ability to communicate effectively.

Speaking skills allow students to become more confident at speaking out loud, and to engage with the English language competently.

Having a strong understanding of the English language will allow students to become fluent in written and spoken English. This will allow them to communicate effectively with the world around them, thus allowing children to become engaged in cultural, social and economic issues, as well as intellectual debates.

ENGLISH SUBJECT CONTENT

Below I have broken down the aims and objectives of each 'discipline' for the subject. This will hopefully give you some idea of what will be assessed, and how you can improve different areas in your reading, writing and speaking abilities.

READING

<u>Pupils will be taught how to:</u>

❏ Develop an appreciation of the English language.
❏ Engage with a variety of literary texts including:
  - *Non-fiction, fiction, plays and poetry. Texts that cover a wide range of genres, eras, authors, styles and narratives.*
  - *Reading books for pleasure and academia.*
  - *Understanding the importance of Shakespeare's works.*
❏ Engage with challenging texts by:
  - *Learning new vocabulary, grammar and literary techniques.*
  - *Analysing key words and phrases.*
  - *Making inferences and assumptions based on the information provided.*
  - *Knowing the meaning behind the text, including the purpose, audience and context.*
❏ Read critically:
  - *Recognising different literary techniques.*
  - *Analysing narration, characterisation, style, themes and genre.*
  - *Comparing two or more texts (cross-examination).*
  - *Understanding meaning through figurative language, word choices, structure and conventions.*

WRITING

<u>Pupils will be taught how to:</u>

❑ Write with fluency, ease and control.
❑ Write a range of different literary texts including:
- *Strong, persuasive, narrative essays.*
- *Short stories, plays and poetry.*
- *Imaginative writing.*
- *Formal letters.*
- *Scripts and presentations.*
❑ Plan, draft and proofread writing:
- *Plan and draft your ideas. Think about:*
  - *Characters, narrative, themes, motives, style, context, audience and purpose.*
- *Carefully choosing grammar and understanding the importance of vocabulary.*
- *Structuring your writing format in a clear and concise manner.*
- *Understanding the importance of audience, and how your writing can be influential.*
❑ Be original and creative.
❑ Use the English language in a way that is expressive, creative, informative, imaginative or personal.

SPOKEN ENGLISH

<u>Pupils will be taught how to:</u>

❑ Verbally communicate to a high standard by:
- *Speaking confidently, persuasively and effectively.*
❑ Improve their speaking skills by engaging with particular grammar and vocabulary:
- *Understanding what type of spoken English they should use and in what context.*
- *Understanding how to get their point across in the best possible way.*
❑ Participate in verbal debates, discussions and presentations.
❑ Improve speaking skills such as volume, tone, enthusiasm and interaction.

GRAMMAR AND VOCABULARY

<u>Pupils will be taught how to:</u>

❏ Improve pre-existing grammar and vocabulary skills taught in Key Stage 2.
❏ Understand the importance of grammar:
  - *How this creates meaning.*
  - *The impact this has on the audience.*
❏ Analyse key words and phrases:
  - *Why they are used.*
  - *The meaning behind them.*
  - *What is the author implying/inferring?*
❏ Understand what grammar and vocabulary to use. Think about:
  - *What kind of literary text they are writing/reading.*
  - *What do words mean and how can they be interpreted?*
  - *Is it a formal or informal piece of literary text?*

English is not only a core subject, but a topic that impacts upon every aspect of our daily lives. As you can see, it is imperative that students are able to engage with the English language, in order to develop key life skills.

USING THIS GUIDE

This guide focuses specifically on Key Stage 3 English Reading (Fiction, Plays & Poetry). This book will focus on the basics that every child will need to know, to ensure top marks in English reading.

HOW WILL I BE ASSESSED?

In Key Stage 3, children will be assessed based on Levels. These years do not count towards anything, and are simply a reflection of progression and development. The first years of secondary school are in place in order to determine whether or not pupils are meeting the minimum requirements, and are integral for preparing pupils for their GCSE courses.

Although these years do not count towards any final results, they do go a long way to deciphering which GCSEs you will pick up. For example, if you were

excelling in Art and Design in KS3, you could consider taking this subject at GCSE. The subjects that you choose at GCSE will impact upon your future aspirations, including further education and career opportunities.

You will be monitored and assessed throughout these schooling years, via the following:

- Ongoing teacher assessments;
- Term progress reports;
- Summative assessments at the end of each academic year.

By the end of Key Stage 3, pupils are expected to achieve Levels 5 or 6.

INCREASE YOUR CHANCES

Below is a list of GOLDEN NUGGETS that will help you and your child to prepare for Key Stage 3 English.

Golden Nugget 1 – Revision timetables

When it comes to revising, preparation is key. That is why you need to sit down with your child and come up with an efficient and well-structured revision timetable.

It is important that you work with your child to assess their academic strengths and weaknesses, in order to carry out these revision sessions successfully.

> *TIP – Focus on their weaker areas first!*
>
> *TIP – Create a weekly revision timetable to work through different subject areas.*
>
> *TIP – Spend time revising with your child. Your child will benefit from your help and this is a great way for you to monitor their progress.*

Golden Nugget 2 – Understanding the best way your child learns

There are many different ways to revise when it comes to exams, and it all comes down to picking a way that your child will find most useful.

Below is a list of the common learning styles that you may want to try with your child:

- **Visual** – the use of pictures and images to remember information.
- **Aural** – the use of sound and music to remember information.
- **Verbal** – the use of words, in both speech and writing, to understand information.
- **Social** – working together in groups.
- **Solitary** – working and studying alone.

Popular revision techniques include: *mind mapping, flash cards, making notes, drawing flow charts,* and *diagrams.* You could instruct your child on how to turn diagrams and pictures into words, and words into diagrams. Try as many different methods as possible, to see which style your child learns from the most.

TIP – Work out what kind of learner your child is. What method will they benefit from the most?

TIP – Try a couple of different learning aids and see if you notice a change in your child's ability to understand what is being taught.

Golden Nugget 3 – Break times

Allow your child plenty of breaks when revising.

It's really important not to overwork your child.

TIP – Practising for 10 to 15 minutes per day will improve your child's reading ability.

TIP – Keep in mind that a child's retention rate is usually between 30 to 50 minutes. Any longer than this, and your child may start to lose interest.

Golden Nugget 4 – Practice, practice and more practice!

Purchase past practice papers. Although the curriculum will have changed for 2016, practice papers are still a fantastic way for you to gain an idea of how your child is likely to be tested.

Golden Nugget 5 – Variety is key!

Make sure that your child reads a VARIETY of different literary texts. Broadening their understanding of different genres, styles and formats will help them prepare effectively for reading an array of literature.

> *TIP – Take your child to a library and let them discover different types of books. This will greatly increase their understanding of different literary styles.*

Golden Nugget 6 – Improve their confidence

Encourage your child to communicate verbally, as well as in writing. This will allow them to improve their confidence and improve their spoken English.

> *TIP – Have discussions and debates in order to encourage your child to open up and discuss their views.*
>
> *TIP – Try and get your child to deliver presentations to family members and friends. This will really help to improve their confidence.*

Golden Nugget 7 – Stay positive!

The most important piece of preparation advice we can give you, is to make sure that your child is positive and relaxed about these tests.

Don't let assessments worry you, and certainly don't let them worry your child.

> *TIP – Make sure the home environment is as comfortable and relaxed as possible for your child.*

Golden Nugget 8 – Answer the easier questions first

A good tip to teach your child is to answer all the questions they find easiest first. That way, they can swiftly work through the paper, before attempting the questions they struggle with.

TIP – Get your child to undergo a practice paper. Tell them to fill in the answers that they find the easiest first. That way, you can spend time helping your child with the questions they find more difficult.

Spend some time working through the questions they find difficult and make sure that they know how to reach the correct answer.

Golden Nugget 9 – Make sure they refer back to the text

One of the biggest mistakes a child can make in their Reading test, is that they don't refer back to the text. All of the answers can be found in the text, therefore they should support their answers with information taken from the passage, as opposed to relying on their memory.

Golden Nugget 10 – Understanding key terms

The next section is a glossary containing all the KEY TERMS that your child should familiarise themselves with.

Sit down with your child and learn as many of these KEY TERMS as you can.

TIP – Why not make your child's learning fun? Write down all of the key terms and cut them out individually. Do the same for the definitions.

Get your child to try and match the KEY TERM with its definition. Keep playing this game until they get them all right!

Golden Nugget 11 – Check out our other revision resources

We have a range of other English resources to help you prepare for EVERY element of KS3 English.

LEARN YOUR
KEY TERMS
(A to Z)

ADJECTIVE	A 'describing' word. A word used to describe how something looks, feels, smells or tastes. Adjectives also tell us how someone is feeling. *Example 1 – An **early** start* *Example 2 – A **large** spider*
ADVERB	Adverbs are words that describe a verb. These words tend to tell us how something or someone is doing, or what they are doing. *Example 1 – The boy walked **slowly*** *Example 2 – He **gracefully** took her hand*
ANTONYM	An antonym refers to a word which has the **opposite** meaning to another. *Example 1 – **Soft** is the antonym of **hard*** *Example 2 – **Up** is the antonym of **down***
APOSTROPHE (')	An apostrophe is a punctuation mark used to (1) indicate belonging or (2) indicate the omission of letters. *Example 1 – Katie's bedroom, Joe's homework* *Example 2 – didn't (did not), can't (cannot), I'm (I am)*
AUDIENCE	The people who view the text.
CHARACTERISATION	The way in which a character is conveyed. Characterisation is the way in which people speak, behave and look.
CLAUSE	A clause is part of a sentence that contains a verb and a subject. *Example 1 – Peter **tackles** (verb) **Jason** (subject)* *Example 2 – Mikey **piggybacks** Jackie*
CLOSE READING	A close, intense reading of a text.

COLON **(:)**	A punctuation mark used to (1) join sentences, (2) introduce lists, (3) introduce a quotation or (4) introduce explanations. *Example 1 – Here is my shopping list: bread, milk, eggs and butter* *Example 2 – Tim was feeling tired: he didn't sleep very well last night*
COMMA **(,)**	A punctuation mark used to indicate (1) a pause between parts of sentences or (2) separating items in list format. *Example 1 – On Tuesday, it was raining* *Example 2 – At the shop, I bought a sausage roll, a packet of crisps, an orange and a chocolate bar*
COMPARING TEXTS	Comparing two or more literary texts, to analyse the similarities and differences.
CONJUNCTION	A conjunction is a word that joins phrases or words together. *Example 1 – I don't like pizza **or** pasta* *Example 2 – Fred loves golf **and** football*
CONTEXT	Historical or cultural context. Understanding the context behind the written text.
CONTRACTION	Contractions are 'shorthand' ways of writing words. It is one word usually made up of two words. *Example 1 – **you've** (you have)* *Example 2 – **doesn't** (does not)*
CRITICAL READING	Reading a text and undergoing critical analysis.
DASH **(–)**	A dash is used to separate information. It is stronger than a comma, but not as formal as a colon. Not to be confused with a hyphen (a dash line is longer).

DETERMINER	A determiner is a word that goes before a noun in order to clarify it. *Example 1 – The party is at **my** house* *Example 2 – I teach a **one** day training course*
ELLIPSIS **(...)**	An ellipsis is a set of three dots (full stops) which can add suspense, leave a sentence hanging or show interruptions or missing words. *Example 1 – Josie stepped outside her front door, when all of a sudden...* *Example 2 – She was without hope... empty...*
EXCLAMATION MARK **(!)**	An exclamation mark is used to show a command or something that is forceful or surprising. *Example 1 – Ouch!* *Example 2 – That really hurt!*
FIGURATIVE LANGUAGE	A way of creating imagery through the use of metaphors, similes, hyperboles, etc.
FULL STOP **(.)**	A full stop should be used to end a sentence. *Example 1 – The dog runs across the road.* *Example 2 – Sam likes peanuts.*
HOMONYMS	These are words that *sound* and are spelled the same, but have different meanings. *Example 1 – **watch** (to watch something) or a watch (to tell the time)* *Example 2 – **fair** (fair skinned) or fair (it's not fair)*
HOMOPHONES	These are words that *sound* the same but are spelt differently, and have different meanings. *Example 1 – **to, too, two*** *Example 2 – **they're, their, there***

INVERTED COMMAS (" ")	Inverted commas are used to show direct speech or quotation. These can either be single (') or double ("). Inverted commas can also be used to draw attention to something unusual, ironic or arguably incorrect. *Example 1 – "What time does the lesson start?"* *Example 2 – Gareth said, "I like theme parks"*
LANGUAGE	The words and vocabulary used in a literary text.
NARRATIVE	The storyline and/or meaning of a text.
NOUN	A word that names something. *Examples – Hannah, London, forest, wolf*
PLURAL	More than one of something. *Examples – toys, teeth, lives, babies*
PREFIX	A prefix is added to the beginning of a word to make a new word. *Example 1 – **dis**regard, **dis**belief* *Example 2 – **un**natural, **un**happy*
PREPOSITION	A preposition tells us where something is or how they are related. *Examples – under, over, before, beside, between, near, beyond, past, from, on top of*
PRONOUN	A word that replaces the noun. *Examples – I, me, she, him, they, which, who, ours, yours, its*
PURPOSE	The reasons why a text was written. Is it to entertain, inform, instruct, persuade, etc?
QUESTION MARK (?)	A question mark is used to show a question. *Example 1 – What time is it?* *Example 2 – How long are you going to be?*

SCANNING	Quickly reading a text in order to find specific information.
SEMI-COLON (;)	A semi-colon is used to separate longer sentences but still reads as one complete sentence. Or to link two closely related sentences. *Example 1 – Polly loves her new trainers; she wears them everywhere* *Example 2 – For Christmas, we spent a day with our grandparents in Ireland; then we spent a day with our aunt and uncle; and then we spent the rest of it back home*
SHAKESPEARE	An English poet and playwright who wrote important sonnets and plays.
SKIMMING	Quickly looking over a text in order to get a general overview of what it is about.
STRUCTURE	The way a literary text is laid out. The structure of a text will depend on what *type* of text it is.
SUFFIX	A suffix is added to the end of the word to make a new word. *Example 1 – charge**able**, manage**able*** *Example 2 – sham**eful**, doubt**ful***
SYNONYM	A word that has the same, or similar, meaning to another word. *Example 1 – pretty = beautiful, stunning, gorgeous* *Example 2 – big = huge, gigantic, enormous, large*
THEMES	The major or subtle ideas that an author explores in the text.
VERB	A verb is a doing or action word. *Example 1 – She **went** to the party* *Example 2 – She **ran** to the shops*

UNDERSTANDING FICTION

(Reading Fiction)

UNDERSTANDING FICTION

WHAT IS FICTION?

Fiction is the creation of stories and ideas. They are created by the IMAGINATION.

These stories did NOT happen in real life.

TYPES OF FICTION

There are many different types, or **genres**, of fiction:

Fantasy	Romance	Horror	Science Fiction (Sci-Fi)
Mystery	Realistic	Historical	Folktales
Adventure	Sports	Humour	Classics

Some fiction stories use more than one **genre**, and this is called a **hybrid**.

UNDERSTANDING FICTION

EXAMPLES OF CLASSIC CHILDREN'S FICTION

There are so many children's books out there by different authors, from different genres.

Entering the world of imagination and original thought will allow children to expand on their own creative ideas.

Listed below are some of the most classic children's fiction books. When you have some time, it is recommended that you read some of these before your English assessments.

Alice in Wonderland	Treasure Island	The Railway Children	Black Beauty
A Little Princess	The Secret Garden	The Wizard of Oz	The Lion, the Witch, and the Wardrobe
Peter Pan	Watership Down	The Indian in the Cupboard	Charlotte's Web
The Borrowers	Annie	Wind in the Willows	Charlie and the Chocolate Factory

THE NARRATIVE

When reading a story it is important, as the reader, to be drawn into the mind-set of the author. For the moments you sit there reading, you want to be able to escape from real life and enter a world full of fantasy and make-believe.

As the creator of fiction, you want to be able to tell a story that is worthwhile and will engage your audience.

Every good fiction book comes with:

- *A creative imagination;*
- *An original idea;*
- *A strong narrative;*
- *Characters that people can relate to, disapprove of, or admire;*
- *An ability to look beyond reality and enter a world of vision, fantasy, and invention.*

UNDERSTANDING FICTION

THE IMPORTANCE OF NARRATIVE

Behind every great fiction book is a strong narrative that draws the reader in, and captures a story that is thrilling and appealing to its targeted readers.

The narrative is where the author can get really creative. Remember, fiction writing is all about fantasy and make-believe. Therefore, the ideas and imagination behind these stories can be completely unrealistic and wacky.

QUESTIONING THE NARRATIVE

It is important that, after reading the text, you think about what has been said.

You need to be able to read an extract from a book, and understand the passage in further detail.

By asking questions as you go through, this will allow you to understand what the author was trying to say:

- *How does the author want me to feel at this point?*
- *How does the author feel at this point?*
- *Why have I been provided this information?*
- *What can I learn from the information that has been provided?*
- *Why has the author used a particular phrase?*
- *Who is the narrator of the text and how are they being portrayed?*

UNDERSTANDING FICTION

STRUCTURE OF FICTION WRITING

All fiction writing will follow a similar structure, and have a beginning, a middle, and an end.

If you are creating your own story, or you are analysing the structure of a narrative, you should consider the following points:

BEGINNING

- Introducing your reader to your style of writing.
- Setting up the scene and introducing the main characters.
- Creating a 'situation' or 'problem' right at the beginning will make sure that your reader is instantly 'hooked'.
- You need to grab the reader's attention. Make it thrilling. Make it fast-paced. Make the reader want to continue reading.
- Don't give away all of the key details at the beginning. Provide your readers with enough information, so that they will want to continue reading on to find out more.

MIDDLE

- This is where the bulk of your story will take place.
- You need to hold the reader's attention by maintaining a plotline that is interesting, and will push the reader to finish the story.
- Develop obstacles and complications which the characters need to solve.
- Although there might be a few complications, your story should reach a CLIMAX or turning point.
- There is a massive situation which the main character has to try and resolve.
- A good middle will allow the reader to wonder how the story will end.

END

- This is where the climax or turning point of your story will become resolved.
- Your main character/s will have learnt a lesson, or come to terms with the events that have happened.
- A good ending will allow the reader to continue thinking about the story, even after finishing reading it.

story

ACTIVITIES

Read a fiction book. This book can be from any genre or author.

Using our template below, paraphrase some key points from the beginning, the middle, and the end of the story.

When writing your notes, not only should you focus on the structure of the narrative, but you should also consider the following:

- Language
- Imagery
- Mood
- Setting
- Atmosphere
- Characterisation
- Themes

BEGINNING

MIDDLE

MIDDLE

END

ACTIVITIES

Why not have a go at structuring your own story?

PRACTICE WRITING

For this exercise, you will need to come up with a suitable title and storyline about anything you want. What you need to do is fill in the boxes below in order to come up with a plan for a possible narrative.

This is a great way to practice for your reading and writing assessments.

TITLE

IDEAS

THEMES / MOTIFS

SETTINGS

CHARACTERS

NARRATIVE

NARRATIVE

SETTING, ATMOSPHERE & EMOTION

(Reading Fiction)

SETTING, ATMOSPHERE & EMOTION

THE IMPORTANCE OF SETTING

The setting of a novel is one of the key elements in literary writing. When writing about settings, you can include descriptions on:

- Where the action takes place;
- What the weather is like;
- What time of day it is.

It is up to the reader how they picture the setting. Everyone visualises stories differently. One thing may look completely different to two different people.

Take a look at the pictures!

Both images are of a forest. However, they both look very different. The way this setting would be described would depend on what feelings, mood and atmosphere the writer was trying to create.

For example, in the first image, it could represent:

- Idealism;
- Peacefulness;
- Beauty.

However, the second image could represent:

- The unknown;
- Fears;
- Isolation.

SETTING, ATMOSPHERE & EMOTION 

CREATING AN ATMOSPHERE AND ADDING EMOTION

When writers describe a setting, they are trying to create a particular mood or atmosphere.

When looking at atmosphere, you should look at:

- What feelings/moods are created?
- How does the atmosphere tie in with the action?
- How does the atmosphere tie in with the narrative?

Different atmospheres created in a story will make the reader *feel* different things. The writing needs to make the reader feel a certain way in order for them to feel engaged with the narrative.

TYPES OF EMOTIONS

The type of emotion that is conveyed in the narrative will depend on what genre the story is from. It will also depend on what is happening at the time (i.e. what action is currently taking place in the narrative?)

There are a whole range of emotions that writers can convey in their writing. This might include some of the following:

Anger	Desire	Wonder	Sorrow
Fear	Guilt	Happiness	Joy
Shame	Love	Envy	Courage
Hope	Confusion	Relaxation	Ghostly

SETTING, ATMOSPHERE & EMOTION

Take a look at the images below!

For each one, write some keywords that you would associate with the image. What mood/atmosphere is created? What action would take place here? How does the image make you feel?

KEYWORDS

KEYWORDS

KEYWORDS

KEYWORDS

QUICK ACTIVITIES

Below are a few words or phrases. Read the word, and draw a quick sketch to try and demonstrate that emotion/situation.

LOST

BRAVERY

FEAR

Jane Eyre by Charlotte Bronte

The red-room was a square chamber, very seldom slept in, I might say never, indeed, unless when a chance influx of visitors at Gateshead Hall rendered it necessary to turn to account all the accommodation it contained: yet it was one of the largest and stateliest chambers in the mansion. A bed supported on massive pillars of mahogany, hung with curtains of deep red damask, stood out like a tabernacle in the centre; the two large windows, with their blinds always drawn down, were half shrouded in festoons and falls of similar drapery; the carpet was red; the table at the foot of the bed was covered with a crimson cloth; the walls were a soft fawn of colour with a blush of pink in it; the wardrobe, the toilet-table, the chairs were of darkly polished old mahogany. Out of these deep surrounding shades rose high, and glared white, the piled-up mattresses and pillows of the bed, spread with a snowy Marseilles counterpane. Scarcely less prominent was an amble cushioned easy-chair near the head of the bed, also white, with a footstool before it; and looking, as I thought, like a pale throne.

The room was chill, because it seldom had a fire; it was silent, because remote from the nursery and kitchen; solemn, because it was known to be so seldom entered. The house-maid alone came here on Saturdays, to wipe from the mirrors and the furniture a week's quiet dust: and Mrs. Reed herself, at far intervals, visited it to review the contents of a certain secret drawer in the wardrobe, where were stored divers parchments, her jewel-casket, and a miniature of her deceased husband; and in those last words lies the secret of the red-room – the spell which kept it so lonely in spite of its grandeur.

Mr. Reed had been dead nine years: it was in this chamber he breathed his last; here he lay in state; hence his coffin was borne by the undertaker's men; and, since that day, a sense of dreary consecration had guarded it from frequent intrusion.

QUESTION 1

What colour does Bronte use to describe the room?

QUESTION 2

List all of the words used to describe the colour of the room.

QUESTION 3

What connotations do you think are attached with the colour of this room?

QUESTION 4

Why do you think Bronte describes the room as being "chill"? Use a quote from the extract to emphasise this idea of coldness.

QUESTION 5

By reading the word "I", it automatically draws you into the narrative. How does the setting of the narrative make YOU feel?

____

____

____

____

QUESTION 6

"Mr. Reed had been dead nine years: it was in this chamber he breathed his last."

Describe the atmosphere this sentence creates.

____

____

____

____

____

____

____

QUESTION 7

The word "stateliest" can be defined as…

Nationalist ☐

Grandest ☐

Expensive ☐

Messiest ☐

QUESTION 8

In the extract, the author uses a simile. Write the simile and explain why the author has made this comparison.

Simile = ____

____

____

____

> *The Wonderful Wizard of Oz* by L. Frank Baum

Dorothy lived in the midst of the great Kansas prairies, with Uncle Henry, who was a farmer, and Aunt Em, who was the farmer's wife. Their house was small, for the lumber to build it had to be carried by wagon many miles. There were four walls, a floor and a roof, which made one room; and this room contained a rusty looking cookstove, a cupboard for the dishes, a table, three or four chairs, and the beds. Uncle Henry and Aunt Em had a big bed in one corner, and Dorothy a little bed in another corner. There was no garret at all, and no cellar – except a small hole dug in the ground, called a cyclone cellar, where the family could go in case one of those great whirlwinds arose, mighty enough to crush any building in its path. It was reached by a trap door in the middle of the floor, from which a ladder led down into the small, dark hole.

When Dorothy stood in the doorway and looked around, she could see nothing but the great grey prairie on every side. Not a tree nor a house broke the broad sweep of flat country that reached to the edge of the sky in all directions. The sun had baked the plowed land into a gray mass, with little cracks running through it. Even the grass was not green, for the sun had burned the tops of the long blades until they were the same gray colour to be seen everywhere. Once the house had been painted, but the sun blistered the paint and the rains washed it away, and now the house was as dull and gray as everything else.

When Aunt Em came there to live she was a young, pretty wife. The sun and wind had changed her, too. They had taken the sparkle from her eyes and left them a sober gray; they had taken the red from her cheeks and lips, and they were gray also. She was thin and gaunt, and never smiled now. When Dorothy, who was an orphan, first came to her, Aunt Em had been so startled by the child's laughter that she would scream and press her hand upon her heart whenever Dorothy's merry voice reached her ears; and she still looked at the little girl with wonder that she could find anything to laugh at.

QUESTION 1

In this extract, L. Frank Baum explores the emotion of feeling isolated. Write down 3 quotes from the passage that highlights this idea.

Quote 1

____

____

Quote 2

____

____

Quote 3

____

____

QUESTION 2

L. Frank Baum writes a great deal about colour imagery in this scene. Why is the colour imagery important, and what atmosphere does this create?

____

____

____

____

____

____

____

____

____

QUESTION 3

"There were four walls, a floor and a roof, which made one room; and this room contained a rusty looking cookstove, a cupboard for the dishes, a table, three or four chairs, and the beds. Uncle Henry and Aunt Em had a big bed in one corner, and Dorothy a little bed in another corner."

Describe the atmosphere of this setting. If you was in this setting, how would it make you feel?

____

____

____

____

____

____

____

____

QUESTION 4

"She still looked at the little girl with wonder that she could find anything to laugh at."

What does this say about Dorothy's surroundings?

____

____

____

____

____

____

____

QUESTION 5

Why do you think L. Frank Baum chose to set his opening scene in the countryside?

____

____

____

____

QUESTION 6

Compare the descriptions of the sun and rain, and how this links to monotonous themes of isolation and dullness.

____

____

____

____

____

____

QUESTION 7

Why do you think the writer has included the word "whirlwind" in relation to emotion and atmosphere?

____

____

____

____

QUESTION 8

Use the first paragraph from the extract from *The Wonderful Wizard of Oz*, and rewrite it, so that you create a more colourful, optimistic picture.

<u>You will be assessed on your grammar, punctuation and spelling. Additional paper may be required.</u>

Footsteps by How2Become

A horrifying cry echoed through the crisp, night air. My heart leapt out of my chest. Every which way looked the same. I was surrounded, trapped by tall trees that barricaded me in this spacious, yet confining place. I stood in the mid of the darkness, as I began to feel a terrifying sense of defeat.

I tried to catch my breath. I thought about running. But where to? I was totally lost. Leaves and twigs crunched beneath my toes. The place was a maze; a maze of uncertainty, a maze of fear, a maze of insanity.

Footsteps.

Count to five, I reassured myself. I remembered a trick my mum used to teach me back at home whenever I was scared. *Count to five.* In those five quick seconds, I would let myself fear the worse. After that, I would take one deep breath and compose myself. I closed my eyes.

One... Two...

Footsteps.

I opened one eye and peered into the emptiness. Nothing.

Three... Four...

Closer and closer.

One sudden swipe across my head and I fell limp, graciously falling to the floor.

QUESTION 1

Why do you think the writer has not identified the exact whereabouts of the setting?

____

____

____

____

____

QUESTION 2

Out of the following, which genre do you think this extract is taken from? Tick one.

Comedy

Romance

Sci-Fi

Drama

Horror

QUESTION 3

Using your answer to question 2, explain why you picked that genre.

____

____

____

____

QUESTION 4

*"The place was a maze; a maze of uncertainty, a maze of fear,
a maze of insanity."*

Why do you think the writer has repeated the word "maze"? What does this signify in terms of emotion?

____

____

____

____

QUESTION 5

*"I was surrounded, trapped by tall trees that barricaded me in this spacious,
yet confining place."*

The words "spacious" and "confining" have opposite meanings. What do you think the writer is trying to say by saying a place is both "spacious" and "confining"?

____

____

____

____

QUESTION 6

The extract is set during the night. Do you think a daylight setting would have the same effect? Explain your answer.

____

____

____

____

QUESTION 7

List all of the emotions that you feel when reading through this extract.

QUESTION 8

Write the next two paragraphs for this story. Remember, try to convey the same emotion and themes as displayed in the extract.

<u>You will be assessed on your grammar, punctuation and spelling.</u>

ANSWERS TO SETTING, ATMOSPHERE & EMOTION

JANE EYRE

Q1.

Red.

Q2.

Red, deep red, crimson, blush of pink.

Q3.

The colour of red connotes this idea of mystery, blood, danger, desire, passion or power. There are lots of other connotations of the colour red, but from this extract it mostly connotes an intense feeling that possibly something bad or emotional has happened in the room.

Q4.

Bronte describes the room as being "chill" because it demonstrates how the room has been left deserted and empty. The "chill" could also imply a chilling feeling, as if someone is on edge being in the room. A chill could also suggest a ghostly figure.

Q5.

This answer would be based on your personal feelings. How does the narrative make YOU feel? Remember to support your answer with reasoning and examples.

Q6.

The fact that a person died in the room creates an intense and ghostly atmosphere. The author also draws on these feelings by stating that the room has a "chill", which again implies an eerie atmosphere.

Considering that "Mr. Reed had been dead nine years" implies how the room has been left unattended ever since, and therefore has built up a sense of abandonment.

Q7.

Grandest.

Q8.

"Scarcely less prominent was an amble cushioned easy-chair near the head of the bed, also white, with a footstool before it; and looking, as I thought, like a pale throne."

This simile emphasises the grandness of the contents of the room, almost making it sound like a room for a royalty.

THE WONDERFUL WIZARD OF OZ

Q1.

Quote 1 = *"Their house was small, for the lumber to build it had to be carried by wagon many miles."*

Quote 2 = *"Not a tree nor a house broke the broad sweep of flat country that reached to the edge of the sky in all directions."*

Quote 3 = *"There were four walls, a floor and a roof, which made one room; and this room contained a rusty looking cookstove, a cupboard for the dishes, a table, three or four chairs, and the beds."*

Q2.

L. Frank Baum uses colour imagery to emphasise the key themes of isolation, entrapment and dullness. The use of the word "gray" is repeatedly used to reiterate the dullness and monotonous atmosphere. This suggests that Dorothy's childhood has been less than joyous.

The use of the colour also connotes 'dingy' and 'loss'. Maybe the writer is trying to emphasise Dorothy's loss of her childhood, or the fact that she feels isolated from experience and the greater world.

Q3.

This response is based on your personal feelings. You need to describe how this quote makes YOU feel. Does it suggest confinement? Why could this be important? How would this atmosphere make you feel?

Q4.

The fact that Dorothy can still find something to laugh about suggests her personality to be optimistic and still child-like. Children are able to find the fun and laughter in little things. It could also suggest that Dorothy has hope and dreams; she wants to experience bigger and better things.

Q5.

The countryside is a great place to set a scene if you wish to convey confinement, solitary and a lack of experience. The setting suggests how Dorothy's upbringing has been far from many experiences. The fact that her house is away from everything suggests how the rest of the narrative could see her explore the wider world.

Q6.

The author draws on the imagery of rain and sun to emphasise the key theme of isolation and monotony. When the writer describes the sun as having "burned the tops of the long blades until they were the same gray colour," this reiterates that even the sun is unable to brighten up the atmosphere of this setting. The rain is used to coincide with the dullness and misery of the setting, and washing away the hopes and brightness of the sun.

FOOTSTEPS

Q1.

The writer has not identified the exact whereabouts of the setting because it helps create this idea of suspense, eeriness and tension. The fact that the reader has no idea where the characters are will entice them to read on further, not only to find out what will happen, but where they are.

Q2.

Horror.

Q3.

The extract is clearly taken from a horror novel. The title, 'Footsteps', poses ideas of fear and the unknown. Hearing footsteps, but not seeing anyone, would be extremely scary. The fact that the opening line begins "a horrifying cry" does not convey a happy or comical start to the narrative. The use of imagery such as darkness, emptiness and loneliness are all key features of a horror story.

Q4.

The use of the word "maze" has been repeated because it emphasises the importance of the unknown. The fact that the place is a maze of uncertainty, fear and insanity, leads the reader to believe that something terrible is going to happen. A maze is a great way to draw the reader in, and represents all sorts of obstacles and troubles.

Q5.

The writer uses the opposite words of "spacious" and "confining" in the same sentence, to suggest that although the setting is large in area, it makes the character feel trapped. This is because the character is not familiar with his/her surroundings, the spaciousness of which ironically makes him/her feel like he/she can't move. The character has no escape route, and is therefore confined to the setting.

Q6.

A daylight setting would not have the same effect as a night-time setting. In a horror story, the main events of a horror will generally take place during the night. This is because it's dark, and is more frightening. A daytime setting is not as eerie or spooky, and therefore will not make the reader feel as on edge or scared.

Q7.

This is based on personal feelings. How does the extract make YOU feel? Why?

Q8.

**This answer requires you to write the next two paragraphs. Try to convey the same emotions and fears as the extract does already.*

This is a great way to assess not only your creative skills, but your ability to write effectively.

Have someone read over your paragraphs. Ask them for feedback, both positive and criticism. This is a great way to learn! Remember, try to add in some literary techniques such as similes, metaphors, personification etc.

HOW ARE YOU GETTING ON?

CHARACTERS & THEMES

(Reading Fiction)

CHARACTERS & THEMES

EVERY GREAT STORY NEEDS GREAT CHARACTERS

The characters of a story are extremely significant as they allow the reader to follow the lives of made-up individuals. The way in which a character comes across to readers is through **characterisation**.

The way a character is **characterised** can be through:

- The way they look;
- The way they speak;
- The way they dress;
- The way they act.

Below are four pictures of different types of characters. For each, write a few keywords about what you would expect their character to be like – consider their appearance, speech, dress code and behaviour/actions.

CHARACTERS & THEMES

THE IMPORTANCE OF THEMES

An author will use one or more themes in their story to emphasise particular ideas.

The genre and narrative of the story will depend on what themes occur.

Below I have listed some of the most common themes:

Love	Hate	Revenge	Jealousy
Justice	Power	Conflict	Childhood
Coming of Age	Struggle	Poverty	Family
Friendship	Death	Courage	Discovery
Ambition	Alienation	Freedom	Fear

Themes are a great way to draw upon emotions.

<u>For example:</u>

- The theme of love connotes happiness and romance;
- The theme of death connotes sadness, anger and isolation.

<u>Some themes can tie in with one another:</u>

- The theme of childhood can also be linked to memories;
- The theme of poverty can also be linked to struggle.

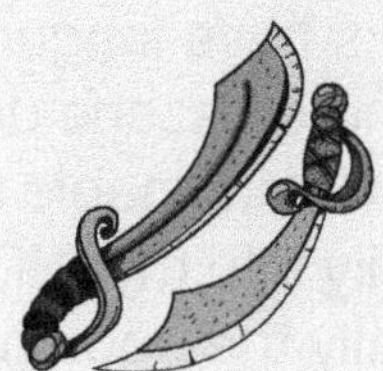

Wuthering Heights by Emily Bronte

The apartment and furniture would have been nothing extraordinary as belonging to a homely, northern farmer, with a stubborn countenance, and stalwart limbs set out to advantage in knee-breeches and gaiters. Such an individual seated in his arm-chair, his mug of ale frothing on the round table before him, is to be seen in any circuit of five or six miles among these hills, if you go at the right time after dinner. But Mr. Heathcliff forms a singular contrast to his abode and style of living. He is a dark-skinned gipsy in aspect, in dress and manners a gentleman: that is, as much a gentlemen as many a country squire: rather slovenly, perhaps, yet not looking amiss with his negligence, because he has an erect and handsome figure; and rather morose. Possibly, some people might suspect him a degree of under-bred pride; I have a sympathetic chord within that tells me it is nothing of the sort: I know, by instinct, his reserve springs from an aversion to showy displays of feeling – to manifestations of mutual kindliness. He'll love and hate equally under cover, and esteem it a species of impertinence to be loved or hated again. No, I'm running on too fast: I bestow my own attributes over-liberally on him. Mr. Heathcliff may have entirely dissimilar reasons for keeping his hand out of the way when he meets a would-be acquaintance, to those which actuate me. Let me hope my constitution is almost peculiar: my dear mother used to say I should never have a comfortable home; and only last summer I proved myself perfectly unworthy of one.

While enjoying a month of fine weather at the sea-coast, I was thrown into the company of a most fascinating creature: a real goddess in my eyes, as long as she took no notice of me. I 'never told my love' vocally; still, if looks have language, the merest idiot might have guessed I was over head and ears: she understood me at last, and looked a return – the sweetest of all imaginable looks. And what did I do? I confess it with shame – shrunk icily into myself, like a snail; at every glance retired colder and farther; till finally the poor innocent was led to doubt her own senses, and, overwhelmed with confusion at her supposed mistake, persuaded her mamma to decamp.

QUESTION 1

Emily Bronte uses a simile in this extract. Write down the simile and explain what this means in terms of personality.

Simile = ____

____

____

____

QUESTION 2

"I 'never told my love' vocally."

What does this say about his character? Why does the writer use inverted commas?

____

____

____

____

QUESTION 3

What themes are conveyed in this extract? Use examples to support your answer.

____

____

____

____

____

____

____

QUESTION 4

Out of the following, which do you think best describes the social class of Mr. Heathcliff? <u>Circle one.</u>

LOWER CLASS   MIDDLE CLASS   UPPER CLASS   MIXTURE

Use examples from the extract to support your answer.

____

____

____

____

____

____

____

____

____

____

____

____

____

QUESTION 5

In your opinion, what do you think Emily Bronte means by "stubborn countenance"?

____

____

____

____

QUESTION 6

Based on this extract, how do you think Mr. Heathcliff represents this idea of a conflicting character?

____

____

____

____

____

____

____

____

____

Alice's Adventures in Wonderland by Lewis Carroll

There seemed to be no use in waiting by the little door, so she went back to the table, half hoping she might find another key on it, or at any rate a book of rules for shutting people up like telescopes: this time she found a little bottle on it, ('which certainly was not here before,' said Alice,) and round the neck of the bottle was a paper label with the words 'DRINK ME' beautifully printed on it in large letters.

It was all very well to say 'Drink me,' but the wise, little Alice was not going to do *that* in a hurry. 'No I'll look first,' she said, 'and see whether it's marked *"poison"* or not:' for she had read several nice little histories about children who had got burnt, and eaten up by wild beasts and other unpleasant things, all because they *would* not remember the simple rules their friends had taught them: such as, that a red-hot poker will burn you if you hold it too long; and that if you cut your finger *very* deeply with a knife, it usually bleeds; and she had never forgotten that, if you drink much from a bottle marked 'poison,' it is almost certain to disagree with you, sooner or later.

However, this bottle was *not* marked 'poison,' so Alice ventured to taste it and finding it very nice, (it had, in fact, a sort of mixed flavour of cherry-tart, custard, pine-apple, roast turkey, toffee, and hot buttered toast,) she very soon finished it off.

'What a curious feeling!' said Alice; 'I must be shutting up like a telescope.'

And so it was indeed: she was now only ten inches high, and her face brightened up at the thought that she was now the right size for going through the little door into that lovely garden. First, however, she waited for a few minutes to see if she was going to shrink any further: she felt a little nervous about this, 'for it might end, you know,' said Alice to herself, 'in my going out altogether like a candle. I wonder what I shall be like then?' And she tried to fancy what the flame of a candle is like after the candle is blown out, for she could not remember ever having seen such a thing.

After a while, finding that nothing more had happened, she decided on going into the garden at once; but alas for poor Alice! When she got to the door, she found she had forgotten the little golden key and when she went back to the table for it, she found she could not possibly reach it: she could see it quite plainly through the glass, and she tried her best to climb up one of the legs of the table, but it was too slippery; and when she had tired herself out with trying, the poor little thing sat down and cried.

'Come, there's no use in crying like that!' said Alice to herself, rather sharply; 'I advise you to leave off this minute!' She generally gave herself very good advice, (though she very seldom followed it), and sometimes she scolded herself so severely as to bring tears into her eyes; and once she remembered trying to box her own ears for having cheated herself in a game of croquet she was playing against herself, for this curious child was very fond of pretending to be two people. 'But it's no use now,' thought poor Alice, 'to pretend to be two people! Why, there's hardly enough of me left to make *one* respectable person!'

QUESTION 1

"It was all very well to say 'Drink me,' but the wise, little Alice was not going to do that in a hurry."

What does this say about Alice's character?

QUESTION 2

How is the theme of curiosity explored?

QUESTION 3

In this extract, Alice speaks a lot to herself. What does this say about the character of Alice?

____

____

____

____

____

____

____

____

____

____

____

QUESTION 4

"'What a curious feeling!' said Alice; 'I must be shutting up like a telescope.'"

What do you think the phrase "shutting up like a telescope" means?

____

____

____

____

____

____

____

QUESTION 5

The author describes how Alice would feel if she was unable to continue her adventures. The author compares this to "what the flame of a candle is like after the candle is blown out". Why do you think the author has made the comparison between Alice's adventures and a burning candle?

QUESTION 6

Lewis Carroll makes reference to change in Alice's size. Why do you think Carroll has done this?

What does this suggest about the character of Alice?

QUESTION 7

Why do you think the writer describes the character of Alice as being conflicted with her inner-self?

QUESTION 8

Do you think Alice should have drunk the potion? Why or why not?

Pride and Prejudice by Jane Austen

Mr. Bingley was good-looking and gentlemanlike: he had a pleasant countenance, and easy, unaffected manners. His sisters were fine women, with an air of decided fashion. His brother-in-law, Mr. Hurst, merely looked the gentleman; but his friend, Mr. Darcy, soon drew the attention of the room by his fine, tall person, handsome features, noble mien, and the report, which was in general circulation within five minutes after his entrance, of his having ten thousand a-year. The gentlemen pronounced him to be a fine figure of a man, the ladies declared he was much handsomer than Mr. Bingley, and he was looked at with great admiration for about half the evening, till his manners gave a disgust which turned the tide of his popularity; for he was discovered to be proud, to be above his company, and above being pleased; and not all his large estate in Derbyshire could then save him from having a most forbidding, disagreeable countenance, and being unworthy to be compared with his friend.

Mr. Bingley had soon made himself acquainted with all the principal people in the room: he was lively and unreserved, danced every dance, was angry that the ball closed so early, and talked of giving one himself at Netherfield. Such amiable qualities must speak for themselves. What a contrast between him and his friend! Mr. Darcy danced only once with Mrs. Hurst and once with Miss. Bingley, declined being introduced to any other lady, and spent the rest of the evening in walking about the room, speaking occasionally to one of his own party. His character was decided. He was the proudest, most disagreeable man in the world, and every body hoped that he would never come there again. Amongst the most violent against him was Mrs. Bennet, whose dislike of his general behaviour was sharpened into particular resentment, by his having slighted one of her daughters.

Elizabeth Bennet had been obliged, by the scarcity of gentlemen, to sit down for two dances; and during part of that time, Mr. Darcy had been standing near enough for her to overhear a conversation between him and Mr. Bingley, who came from the dance for a few minutes to press his friend to join it.

"Come Darcy," said he, "I must have you dance. I hate to see you standing about by yourself in this stupid manner. You had much better dance."

"I certainly shall not. You know how I detest it, unless I am particularly acquainted with my partner. At such an assembly as this, it would be insupportable. Your sisters are engaged, and there is not another woman in the room whom it would not be a punishment to me to stand up with."

"I would not be so fastidious as you are," cried Bingley, "for a kingdom! Upon my honour, I never met with so many pleasant girls in my life as I have this evening; and there are several of them, you see, uncommonly pretty."

"You are dancing with the only handsome girl in the room," said Mr. Darcy, looking at the eldest Miss Bennet.

"Oh, she is the most beautiful creature I ever beheld! But there is one of her sisters sitting down just behind you, who is very pretty, and I dare say very agreeable. Do let me ask my partner to introduce you."

"Which do you mean?" and turning round, he looked for a moment at Elizabeth, till, catching her eye, he withdrew his own, and coldly said, "She is tolerable; but not handsome enough to tempt me; and I am in no humour at present to give consequence to young ladies who are slighted by other men. You had better return to your partner and enjoy her smiles, for you are wasting your time with me."

Mr. Bingley followed his advice. Mr. Darcy walked off; and Elizabeth remained with no cordial feelings towards him. She told the story, however, with great spirit among her friends; for she had a lively, playful disposition, which delighted in any thing ridiculous.

QUESTION 1

Analyse Mr. Darcy's character. How is Darcy represented?

How do you suppose the theme of class inflicts Darcy's personality towards other people, especially women?

QUESTION 2

Discuss the difference in masculinity between Mr. Darcy and Mr. Bingley.

QUESTION 3

Write down some keywords as to how you would describe Mr. Darcy.

QUESTION 4

How is beauty explored in this extract?

QUESTION 5

Analyse the speech in this extract. What does this say about the characters and how do they differ from one another?

QUESTION 6

How are women represented in this extract?

ANSWERS TO CHARACTERS & THEMES

WUTHERING HEIGHTS

Q1.

"I confess it with shame – shrunk icily into myself, like a snail."

The use of the simile compares the behaviour of a human to a snail, by curling up inside its shell in order to hide away and protect itself.

Q2.

The use of the phrase, "I 'never told my love' vocally" suggests the character as being quite reserved. The fact that he did not express his feelings to his 'love' could either indicate several reasons: that he doesn't think she feels the same way, that he feels unworthy of her love, or that he should not have fallen in love with her to begin with. The writer uses inverted commas around 'never told my love' because he was quoting a line from *'Twelfth Night'*, a comedy by William Shakespeare. This is relevant because this play deals with the ups and downs of being in love.

Q3.

*The themes that you could discuss for this question include:

- Love
- Contrasts
- Social class
- Emotion

Use examples to support your answer and explain why they are relevant to the theme you have discussed.

Q4.

Mixture

- "He is a dark-skinned gipsy in aspect, in dress and manners a gentleman".

- "But Mr. Heathcliff forms a singular contrast to his abode and style of living."

- "Possibly, some people might suspect him a degree of under-bred pride."

Q5.

"Stubborn countenance" suggests that Mr. Heathcliff appears to be a man of quite stubborn expressions. The use of the word 'countenance' basically means how he is perceived.

Q6.

Heathcliff is described as a conflicted character.

- "But Mr. Heathcliff forms a singular contrast to his abode and style of living."

- "Possibly, some people might suspect him a degree of under-bred pride."

Why do you think the writer has done this? Why does Heathcliff appear to be of one social class, but act in a different way?

ALICE'S ADVENTURES IN WONDERLAND

Q1.

Alice is described as "wise" in this line for not drinking the potion until she has checked for a label marked "poison". This is an ironic description of Alice, because she does not act wisely – Alice is still very quick to taste the unknown substance, and her check to see if it was poison (or could harm her) was far from rigorous. By doing this, the author conveys how Alice's curiosity far outweighs her caution, and indeed her wisdom.

Q2.

- *"It was all very well to say 'Drink me,' but the wise, little Alice was not going to do THAT in a hurry."*

You could write how Alice showed interest in drinking the bottle and was curious to see what would happen.

- *"When she got to the door, she found she had forgotten the little golden key."*

This shows Alice's curiosity as she is trying to use the door to enter into the unknown.

Q3.

Alice speaks to herself as a sign of showing how lonely her character is. The fact that she is seeking adventures suggests that Alice is not satisfied with her life and wishes to change it. The fact that she talks to herself reminds the reader that Alice only wants companionship, and is young and naïve.

Q4.

The phrase, "shutting people up like telescopes" is most likely referring to making someone smaller. "Shutting up" doesn't necessarily mean to make someone quiet, but to "shut up" i.e. to make smaller, like a telescope when it's put away after being used.

Q5.

The significance of the candle burning out is compared to Alice wanting to finish her adventures. A fading candle represents Alice's feelings if she is unable to continue on with her adventures.

Q6.

The author conveys Alice's character in different sizes – small and normal-sized. This is emphasised when she drinks the potion and shrinks to "ten inches tall". The author does this to illustrate fantasy; "I must be shutting up like a telescope". This could not happen in real life and therefore it's all in the imagination. The author might have done this to show that Alice is not comfortable with who she is. For example, she has to change into a different version of herself in order to find happiness.

Q7.

The author describes the main character, Alice, as someone who is "very fond of pretending to be two people". This could be because Alice is unhappy with who she is, and is trying to be someone else. It shows that Alice has a creative imagination and is able to gain a new perspective.

Q8.

This question relies on personal response. You can choose either yes or no, as long as you support your reasons with evidence from the passage.

<u>*For example:*</u>

You could argue yes for whether Alice should have drunk the potion. You could support your answer by explaining how Alice is a "curious" young girl and seeks adventure. Finding the "key" and unlocking the door is a way of her finding out more about who she is. The use of the word "telescopes" suggests that there is more to see, and she wants to find a new perspective. These are all reasons for why Alice should have drunk the potion.

PRIDE AND PREJUDICE

Q1.

Within this extract, Mr. Darcy is represented as being quite egotistical, headstrong, and upper class. His ability to capture the "attention of the room by his fine, tall person, handsome features [and] noble mien" reinforces how he is a significant character to the narrative. He comes across as quite arrogant and "fastidious" by refusing to participate in the social surroundings. The fact that he undermines women shows that not only does he exert authority, but also shows the conflict between upper and lower classes – he sees himself better than the people he is around.

Q2.

Mr. Darcy and Mr. Bingley are represented in different ways. Masculinity can be analysed within this extract, by both gentlemen exerting their masculinity in different ways. Mr. Darcy is represented as being reserved, egotistical and conceited, withdrawn from anyone who he deems beneath him. In contrast, Mr. Bingley's attempts to 'woo' a woman show how he is less about fortune, and more about companionship and romance. Masculinity is explored by conveying two men; one of which is arrogant, and the other a sociable, polite man who is willing to participate. This exploration makes the reader consider how they personally would define masculinity.

Q3.

This answer will be based on your personal interpretation of the character of Mr. Darcy. For example: arrogant, headstrong, powerful, fastidious, reserved etc.

Q4.

The theme of beauty is explored in this extract most notably through the descriptions of the characters. Mr. Darcy, despite being disliked by most, is considered to be "handsome" and stole the attention of the room. Although Mr. Bingley is also described as "good-looking and gentlemanlike," Mr. Darcy was declared "much handsomer than Mr. Bingley." The way in which Mr. Darcy talks about women is often in terms of beauty. When he speaks with

Mr. Bingley, he claims that Mr. Bingley is "dancing with the only handsome girl in the room." The fact that it would be a "punishment" to dance with anyone else, suggests how picky and egotistical Mr. Darcy's character can be.

Q5.

The way in which Mr. Darcy speaks in this extract is much more conceited compared to that of Mr. Bingley. The fact that Mr. Darcy claims that there is no woman in the room to "tempt [him]" reinforces how his character is deemed of a higher social power. The way in which Mr. Bingley speaks is a huge contrast. He is polite, and chooses to act respectful to everyone, despite of their class. This shows a huge conflict in social class and power.

Q6.

Although the women do not actually speak in this extract, the characters of the sisters obviously play a huge role in the narrative. The fact that Mr. Bingley is dancing with the "most beautiful creature [he] ever beheld" suggests the theme of beauty and grace. However, the character of Elizabeth seems to be quite headstrong for a woman of her time (the 1800s). She told her friends about Mr. Darcy, and demonstrates that beauty and class do not matter to her. She finds Mr. Darcy to be quite an arrogant character, and has no cordial feelings towards him.

HOW ARE YOU GETTING ON?

IMAGERY & LANGUAGE

(Reading Fiction)

IMAGERY & LANGUAGE

IDENTIFYING IMAGERY

When we talk about imagery, it is not always used in a literal sense. More often than not, writers use imagery as a way of describing something in a symbolic way.

Writers will use particular words and phrases to emphasise a particular idea or image in order to create a picture in the reader's imagination.

When looking at imagery, you should ask yourself the following questions:

1. What is the image?
2. How and why is it effective?
3. Can it be interpreted in another way?

There are two main ways that an author can create effective imagery:

IMAGERY & LANGUAGE 

UNDERSTANDING SIMILES

A simile is a sentence that describes something "as" or "like" or "than" something.

> ### She was as white as a ghost.

> ### My brothers were fighting like cat and dog.

She was as white as a ghost.

- The simile compares the appearance of a girl to a ghost.
- The use of the word "as" describes one thing like something else.

My brothers were fighting like cat and dog.

- The simile compares the behaviour of two boys to a cat and dog fighting.
- The use of the word "like" describes the boys' behaviour being similar to the behaviour of a cat and dog fighting.

<u>What similes can you think of?</u>

IMAGERY & LANGUAGE

UNDERSTANDING METAPHORS

A metaphor is a sentence where one thing is called something else. In other words, it is a figure of speech in which a word or phrase is applied to something else, which is not literally applicable.

> ## Life is a roller coaster.

> ## Their bedroom is a zoo.

Life is a roller coaster.

- The metaphor suggests that life has its ups and downs.
- It is comparing life like a roller coaster.
- The fact that it doesn't use the words "as" or "like", means it is a metaphor, and not a simile.

Their bedroom is a zoo.

- The metaphor suggests that their bedroom is a mess and/or chaotic.
- It is comparing a bedroom to a zoo.
- The fact that it doesn't use the words "as" or "like", means it is a metaphor, and not a simile.

<u>What metaphors can you think of?</u>

IMAGERY & LANGUAGE

GETTING TO GRIPS WITH LANGUAGE

Authors are able to get extremely creative in their writing, and tend to use literary techniques to create a certain effect.

There are lots of different literary techniques which can be used – each using language in a different way in order to create meaning or effect.

Below I have outlined some of the key literary techniques that you should familiarise yourself with:

Personification	Repetition	Hyperbole
Emotive language	Onomatopoeia	Pathetic fallacy
Oxymoron	Rhetorical question	Alliteration
Symbolism	Assonance	Colloquialism
Tautology	Bathos	Irony

- Personification

Personification is used to describe inanimate objects or ideas using human or animal-like attributes.

> The wind whispered through the night.

- Repetition

Repetition is when you repeat the same few words or phrases in order to create emphasis.

> Because I can. Because I want to. Because I need to.

IMAGERY & LANGUAGE

- Hyperbole

This is a fancy way of saying 'exaggeration'. Again, this technique is used to create emphasis on a particular idea or word.

> Your bag weighs a ton!

- Emotive language

Writers often use emotive language to evoke feelings and create an impact on the reader.

> An innocent bystander was left in a critical condition after being crushed by a car collision.

- Onomatopoeia

Onomatopoeia is when a word *sounds* like the thing or object it is describing.

> Tom cracked his knuckles.

- Pathetic fallacy

A form of personification in which natural or inanimate objects are given human characteristics.

> It was a tearful night in October.

- Oxymoron

An oxymoron is when words that have opposite meanings are put together in conjunction.

> Hell's angels   Living dead   Act naturally

IMAGERY & LANGUAGE

- Rhetorical question

A rhetorical question is a question that does not require an answer.

> Can't you do anything right?

- Alliteration

Alliteration is when consecutive words begin with the same letter, and sound the same.

> The slithering snake slid through the grass.

- Symbolism

Writers often use symbolism in their writing to convey a certain idea or quality.

> A dove could be symbolic for freedom and purity.

- Assonance

This is when two or more words repeat the same vowel sound in a sentence, but start with different consonants.

> The engin**ee**r held the st**ee**ring wh**ee**l to st**ee**r the vehicle.

- Colloquialism

A word or phrase often used in informal language. For example, slang.

> Go bananas - go crazy or angry.

IMAGERY & LANGUAGE

- Tautology

Tautology is when the same thing is said more than once, using a different way of saying it.

> My first priority is to email my boss.

- Bathos

The anti-climax created by the mood which makes something seem trivial or ridiculous.

> He spoke his final breath in the same inappropriate manner as normal; chatting-up his nurse.

- Irony

An expression which is used to signify the exact opposite.

> A place that prides themselves on always being open, but are closed on the day you turn up.

Can you think of any other language device? What does it mean and how is it used in writing?

Pride and Prejudice by Jane Austen

"I have been used to consider poetry as the *food* of love," said Darcy.

"Of a fine, stout, healthy love it may. Everything nourishes what is strong already. But if it be only a slight, thin sort of inclination, I am convinced that one good sonnet will starve it entirely away."

Darcy only smiled; and the general pause which ensued made Elizabeth tremble lest her mother should be exposing herself again. She longed to speak, but could think of nothing to say; and after a short silence Mrs. Bennet began repeating her thanks to Mr. Bingley for his kindness to Jane, with an apology for troubling him also with Lizzy. Mr. Bingley was unaffectedly civil in his answer, and forced his younger sister to be civil also, and say what the occasion required. She performed her part indeed without much graciousness, but Mrs. Bennet was satisfied, and soon afterwards ordered her carriage. Upon this signal, the youngest of her daughters put herself forward. The two girls had been whispering to each other during the whole visit, and the result of it was, that the youngest should tax Mr. Bingley with having promised on his first coming into the country to give a ball at Netherfield.

Lydia was a stout, well-grown girl of fifteen, with a fine complexion and good-humoured countenance; a favourite with her mother, whose affection had brought her into public at an early age. She had high animal spirits, and a sort of natural self-consequence, which the attention of the officers, to whom her uncle's good dinners, and her own easy manners recommended her, had increased into assurance. She was very equal, therefore, to address Mr. Bingley on the subject of the ball, and abruptly reminded him of his promise; adding, that it would be the most shameful thing in the world if he did not keep it. His answer to this sudden attack was delightful to their mother's ear:

"I am perfectly ready, I assure you, to keep my engagement; and when your sister is recovered, you shall, if you please, name the very day of the ball. But you would not wish to be dancing when she is ill."

Lydia declared herself satisfied. "Oh! Yes – it would be much better to wait till Jane was well, and by that time most likely Captain Carter would be at Meryton again. And when you have given *your* ball," she added, "I shall insist on their giving one also. I shall tell Colonel Forster it will be quite a shame if he does not."

Mrs. Bennet and her daughters then departed, and Elizabeth returned to Jane, leaving her own and her relations' behaviour to the remarks of the two ladies and Mr. Darcy; the latter of whom, however, could not be prevailed on to join in their censure of *her*, in spite of all Miss. Bingley's witticisms on *fine eyes*.

QUESTION 1

"I have been used to consider poetry as the food of love."

What kind of literary technique is this?

QUESTION 2

Using the above quote, describe how the language Darcy uses suggests his character to be of a high social class.

QUESTION 3

What do you think "sonnets" represent? Why do you think the author chooses this type of poem to talk about?

QUESTION 4

What do you think the word "carriage" symbolises?

QUESTION 5

Why do you think Jane Austen describes the character of Lydia as having "animal spirits"?

QUESTION 6

What role does the mother play in this extract?

The Wonderful Wizard of Oz by L. Frank Baum

Then a strange thing happened.

The house whirled around two or three times and rose slowly through the air. Dorothy felt as if she were going up in a balloon.

The north and south winds met where the house stood, and made it the exact center of the cyclone. In the middle of a cyclone the air is generally still, but the great pressure of the wind on every side of the house raised it up higher and higher, until it was at the very top of the cyclone; and there it remained and was carried miles and miles away as easily as you could carry a feather.

It was very dark, and the wind howled horribly around her, but Dorothy found she was riding it quite easily. After the first few whirls around, and one other time when the house tipped badly, she felt as if she were being rocked gently, like a baby in a cradle.

Toto did not like it. He ran about the room, now here, now there, barking loudly but Dorothy sat quite still on the floor and waited to see what would happen.

Once Toto got too near the open trap door, and fell in; and at first the little girl thought she had lost him. But soon she saw one of his ears sticking up through the hole, for the strong pressure of the air was keeping him up so that he could not fall. She crept to the hole, caught Toto by the ear, and dragged him into the room again, afterward closing the trap door so that no more accidents could happen.

Hour after hour passed away, and slowly Dorothy got over her fright; but she felt quite lonely, and the wind shrieked so loudly all about her that she nearly became deaf. At first she had wondered if she would be dashed to pieces when the house fell again; but as the hours passed and nothing terrible happened, she stopped worrying and resolved to wait calmly and see what the future would bring. At last she crawled over the swaying floor to her bed, and lay down upon it; and Toto followed and lay down beside her.

In spite of the swaying of the house and the wailing of the wind, Dorothy soon closed her eyes and fell fast asleep.

QUESTION 1

L. Frank Baum uses two similes. Rewrite these two similes.

Simile 1

____

____

Simile 2

____

____

QUESTION 2

What does a "cyclone" symbolise?

____

____

____

____

____

QUESTION 3

Why do you think the author has written about a "trap door"? What could this symbolise?

____

____

____

____

____

____

QUESTION 4

The author uses personification in his writing. Find two examples and explain why the writer uses this literary technique.

Personification 1

____

Personification 2

____

Explanation of literary technique

____

____

____

QUESTION 5

Why do you think the comparison is made between the rising of the house and a balloon? What does a balloon connote?

____

____

____

____

____

QUESTION 6

How does the writer use alliteration in their work? What impact does this have on the reader?

____

____

____

____

ANSWERS TO IMAGERY & LANGUAGE

PRIDE & PREJUDICE

Q1.

Simile.

Q2.

The term 'poetry' is often considered to be a type of literature most associated with the upper class. The use of technical language and hidden meanings are said to be challenging for lower classes, and is an 'art' that the upper class find desirable. The fact that Mr. Darcy compares poetry to the "food of love" highlights the passion and joy he gets from poetic conventions.

Q3.

Sonnets represent the idea of love, desire and passion. The quote, "I am convinced that one good sonnet will starve it entirely away" suggests that Elizabeth's character only believes love will stay for as long as it is good and strong. The author mentions sonnets because they are mostly related to feelings of love and desire; a feeling of which Elizabeth and Mr. Darcy are conflicted with.

Q4.

The word "carriage" symbolises wealth and the upper class. This prop in the narrative highlights the difference in social classes between the Darcys and the Bennets.

Q5.

Austen describes the character of Lydia as having "animal spirits" because it suggests that she plays a more active, outspoken role than most women within the society of her time. Lydia speaks directly to Mr. Bingley, giving him orders as opposed to suggestions. This reinforces how men and women are being conveyed as sharing a certain level of equality. However, the fact remains that her sisters are more reserved which implies how Lydia's behaviour could be seen as confrontational – challenging the role women are supposed to play in the time this novel was written.

Q6.

The mother in this extract is represented as being quite 'out-there' in regards to finding suitors for her daughters. She makes it abundant that she puts on an act in front of the men in order to make her daughters seem eligible for them. When Elizabeth says something out of line, her mother "tremble[s]", suggesting that she does not agree with her daughter's behaviour. She prizes her daughters on beauty and courage, attributes which men should find desirable.

THE WONDERFUL WIZARD OF OZ

Q1.

Simile 1

"...and there it remained and was carried miles and miles away as easily as you could carry a feather."

Simile 2

"She felt as if she were being rocked gently, like a baby in a cradle."

Q2.

A "cyclone" symbolises disaster. It represents destruction and the feelings of being powerless and unable to control the situation.

Q3.

A "trap door" can symbolise loneliness. It signifies confinement and isolation. This allows us to understand the character of Dorothy in a bit more detail. We realise that Dorothy is 'trapped' and feels isolated from the rest of the world. It also signifies an escape route; the fact that a trap door can be entered into, could be a sign for Dorothy escaping her life and entering a world of adventure.

Q4.

Personification 1 = *"the wind howled horribly around her."*

Personification 2 = *"the wind shrieked so loudly all about her that she nearly became deaf."*

Explanation of literary technique = personification is used to describe inanimate things or ideas using human or animal-like qualities.

Q5.

The comparison between the rising of the house and a balloon is made because it demonstrates how the situation is uncontrollable. If you let go of a balloon, it is going to float away; this is something you cannot stop from happening. This is the same position in which Dorothy finds herself in; she is unable to control the situation which is caused by the cyclone.

Q6.

The writer uses the literary technique of alliteration throughout their work in order to make their writing read more rhythmically. For example, L. Frank Baum uses several alliterations in this extract including, "howled horribly," and "wailing of the wind". This makes these words sound music-like and rhythmic, which allows the reader to create instant images about what is being described.

HOW ARE YOU GETTING ON? 

UNDERSTANDING PLAYS

UNDERSTANDING PLAYS

WHAT IS A PLAY?

A play is a form of literature that is written by a **playwright**, which is intended to be **performed** on stage, radio, TV or film.

The layout of a **script** is really important. Apart from looking aesthetically pleasing, it needs to be clear and *look* like a play script.

A PLAY SCRIPT

A script contains TWO main elements in order to convey the style of a play:

Dialogue

- A conversation between characters. In a literary text, the name of the character always appears on the left side of the page, followed by what they say. Each characters dialogue is written on a separate line.

Stage directions

- Instructions for both the actors and director, usually written in italics or with brackets. These instructions tell the actors how to enter the scene, how they should speak or move, and how props need to be used.

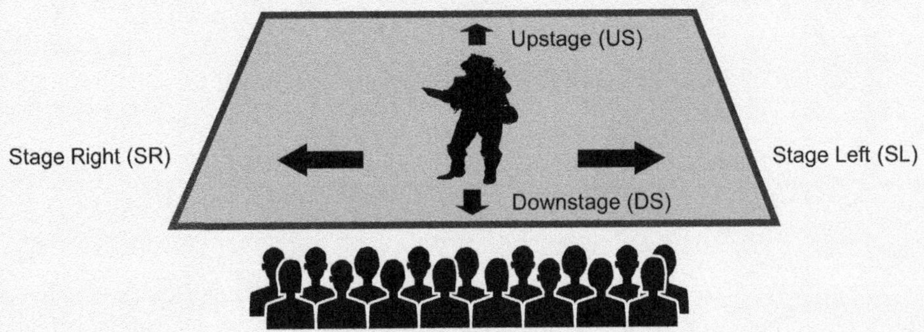

UNDERSTANDING PLAYS

THE STRUCTURE OF A PLAY

A play is broken up into different **scenes**. These scenes act similarly to chapters in a book.

The scenes sometimes allow for an interval/intermission so that the audience and actors can have a break during a live performance.

These scenes make up an **act**.

ACT 1	ACT 2	ACT 3	ACT 4
Scene 1	Scene 1	Scene 1	Scene 1
Scene 2	Scene 2	Scene 2	Scene 2
Scene 3	Scene 3	Scene 3	Scene 3
Scene 4	Scene 4	Scene 4	Scene 4

THINGS TO CONSIDER

Although the layout of the play script is important, there are other things that need to be considered:

Plotline or narrative

- Every successful play needs a great storyline.

Scenery or mise-en-scène

- Everything you see on the set.

Characters

- This includes the number of characters, appearance, body language, how they act;
- **Characterisation** is extremely important when it comes to plays, as the audience need to be able to identify the role of each character. The way a role is characterised is largely down to the actor. They bring the character to life.

Costumes

- The costumes need to reflect the narrative and time in which the play is set.

UNDERSTANDING PLAYS

WILLIAM SHAKESPEARE

William Shakespeare is a hugely important British poet and playwright, and is still considered one of the greatest writers in literary history, even though over 400 years have passed since his time of writing.

SHAKESPEARE AND HIS WORK

Shakespeare wrote around 40 plays, 154 sonnets and a whole range of other poetry.

Some of his most well-known plays include:

Romeo and Juliet	Macbeth	Julius Caesar
A Midsummer Night's Dream	The Taming of the Shrew	Much Ado About Nothing
King Lear	Hamlet	Othello

The works of Shakespeare are taught in schools as a way of recognising writing that is in an old-fashioned style.

Due to the time in which Shakespeare was writing (the 1600s), his writing style was very different to how we read and write today.

Looking at Shakespeare is a great way for children to learn the importance of language in relation to context. The time in which something is written has great bearing on the writing style which is used. Some modern authors use old-fashioned writing techniques to emphasise that their writing is being placed during a different time period.

UNDERSTANDING PLAYS 

TYPES OF SHAKESPEAREAN PLAYS

There are three types of Shakespearean plays:

1. Comedies
2. Tragedies
3. Histories

Comedies

- This is a different type of humour than what we find funny in today's world.
- Most Shakespearean comedies offer dramatic storylines, alongside their underlying humour.
- Most comedies offer a happy ending.

Characteristics = struggle of young love, element of separation, mistaken identities, interwoven plotlines, use of puns and irony and family conflict / tension.

Tragedies

- Tend to be more serious, dramatic and tense.
- Usually involve death of the main character/s.

Characteristics = social breakdown, isolation of main characters, ends in death, noble characters who are brought down by their flaws and no escape from the drama.

Histories

- Focus on English monarchs including King John, Richard II, Henry VIII and loads more.
- Use of Elizabethan propaganda.
- Dangers of civil war and conflict.
- Present a particular image of monarchs, although often considered as misrepresentations and inaccurate.

Characteristics = use of English monarchs to centre the storyline, glorify ancestors, depict monarchs in a particular way, and use conflict and tragedy to dramatise the narrative.

UNDERSTANDING PLAYS

THE USE OF LANGUAGE

Many people struggle to understand the works of Shakespeare, because his writing style and language is extremely different to ours.

The use of old-fashioned language made it difficult for readers to interpret, but these words and phrases were often worked out by understanding the rest of the script.

Example from Romeo and Juliet:

ACT II   **Scene II**   *(Capulet's orchard).*

[Juliet appears above at a window]

ROMEO.   But soft! what light through yonder window breaks?
It is the east and Juliet is the sun.
Arise, fair sun, and kill the envious moon,
Who is already sick and pale with grief
That thou, her maid, art far more fair than she.
Be not her maid, since she is envious;
Her vestal livery is but sick and green,

Shakespeare also used poetry techniques in his plays. The characters in his plays would sometimes speak in a poetic form, and this allows the play to gain rhythm and pace in regards to language and dialogue.

Romeo and Juliet by William Shakespeare

ROMEO

If I profane with my unworthiest hand

This holy shrine, the gentle sin is this:

My lips, two blushing pilgrims, ready stand

To smooth that rough touch with a tender kiss.

JULIET

Good pilgrim, you do wrong your hand too much,

Which mannerly devotion shows in this;

For saints have hands that pilgrims' hands do touch,

And palm to palm is holy palmers' kiss.

ROMEO

Have not saints lips, and holy palmers too?

JULIET

Ay, pilgrim, lips that they must use in prayer.

ROMEO

O, then, dear saint, let lips do what hands do;

They pray; grant thou, lest faith turn to despair.

JULIET

Saints do not move, though grant for prayers' sake.

ROMEO

Then move not, while my prayer's effect I take.

He kisses her.

Thus from my lips, by yours, my sin is purged.

JULIET

Then have my lips the sin that they have took.

ROMEO

Sin from thy lips? O trespass sweetly urged!

Give me my sin again.

They kiss again

QUESTION 1

What imagery is conveyed throughout the passage? How does this appeal to the audience?

QUESTION 2

From the opening of this passage, to when Romeo first kisses Juliet, there are 14 lines of spoken English. How does this convey poetic conventions and what does this tell the audience about their relationship?

QUESTION 3

What does "my unworthiest hand" mean? How does this tie in with family conflict?

QUESTION 4

What do you think Romeo and Juliet are talking about when they are discussing sins in relation to kisses?

The Taming of the Shrew by William Shakespeare

> *Exeunt all but Petruchio.*
> And woo her with some spirit when she comes,
> Say that she rail; why then I'll tell her plain,
> She sings as sweetly as a nightingale:
> Say that she frown; I'll say she looks as clear
> As morning roses newly wash'd with dew:
> Say she be mute and will not speak a word;
> Then I'll commend her volubility,
> And say she uttereth piercing eloquence:
> If she do bid me pack, I'll give her thanks,
> As though she bid me stay by her a week:
> If she deny to wed, I'll crave the day
> When I shall ask the banns, and when be married.
> But here she comes, and now, Petruchio, speak.
> *Enter Katherina*
> Good morrow, Kate; for that's your name, I hear.
>
> **KATHERINA**
> Well have you heard, but something hard of hearing:
> They call me Katherina that do talk to me.
>
> **PETRUCHIO**
> You lie, in faith; for you are call'd plain Kate,
> And bonny Kate, and sometimes Kate the curst;
> But Kate, the prettiest Kate in Christendom,
> Kate of Kate-Hall, my super-dainty Kate,
> For dainties are all Kates, and therefore, Kate,
> Take this of me, Kate of me consolation;
> Hearing thy mildness praised in every town,
> Thy virtues spoke of, and thy beauty sounded,
> Yet not so deeply as to thee belongs,
> Myself am moved to woo thee for my wife.

QUESTION 1

Why do you think Petruchio repeats Kate's name several times?

QUESTION 2

Discuss how Petruchio's attempt to woo Katherina is by counteracting everything she says and does. What does this say about gender roles?

QUESTION 3

When Katherina enters, Petruchio greets her as "Kate". However, Katherina adamantly corrects him and states that everyone calls her "Katherina".

Why do you think Petruchio continues to address her as "Kate"?

QUESTION 4

Describe the power struggles between Katherina and Petruchio.

As You Like It by William Shakespeare

ORLANDO

Why, whither, Adam, wouldst thou have me go?

ADAM

No matter whither, so you come not here.

ORLANDO

What, wouldst thou have me go and beg my food?

Or with a base and boisterous sword enforce

A thievish living on the common road?

This I must do, or know not what to do:

Yet this I will not do, do how I can;

I rather will subject me to the malice

Of a diverted blood and bloody brother.

ADAM

But do not so. I have five hundred crowns,

The thrifty hire I saved under your father,

Which I did store to be my foster-nurse

When service should in my old limbs lie lame

And unregarded age in corners thrown:

Take that, and He that doth the ravens feed,

Yea, providently caters for the sparrow,

Be comfort to my age! Here is the gold;

And all this I give you. Let me be your servant:

Though I look old, yet I am strong and lusty;

For in my youth I never did apply

Hot and rebellious liquors in my blood,

Nor did not with unbashful forehead woo

The means of weakness and debility;

Therefore my age is as a lusty winter,

Frosty, but kindly: let me go with you;

I'll do the service of a younger man
In all your business and necessities.

ORLANDO

O good old man, how well in thee appears
The constant service of the antique world,
When service sweat for duty, not for meed!
Thou art not for the fashion of these times,
Where none will sweat but for promotion,
And having that, do choke their service up
Even with the having: it is not so with thee.
But, poor old man, thou prunest a rotten tree,
That cannot so much as a blossom yield
In lieu of all thy pains and husbandry.
But come thy ways: we'll go along together,
And ere we have thy youthful wages spent,
We'll light upon some settled low content.

ADAM

Master, go on, and I will follow thee,
To the last gasp, with truth and loyalty.
From seventeen years till now almost fourscore
Here lived I, but now live here no more.
At seventeen years many their fortunes seek;
But as fourscore it is too late a week:
Yet fortune cannot recompense me better
Than to die well and not my master's debtor.

    Exit.

QUESTION 1

"I rather will subject me to the malice / Of a diverted blood and bloody brother."

How does this line represent the relationship between Orlando and his brother Oliver?

____

____

____

____

____

____

____

QUESTION 2

"O good old man, how well in thee appears / The constant service of the antique world, / When service sweat for duty, not for meed! / Thou art not for the fashion of these times."

Compare and contrast the views of Shakespeare's language to views of modern day society.

____

____

____

____

____

____

____

QUESTION 3

Describe the relationship between Orlando and Adam.

QUESTION 4

In Adam's speech, beginning with *"Master, go on, and I will follow thee"*, Shakespeare uses verses to emphasise the character as being noble.

Using examples from this extract, explain the importance of Shakespeare's language and how the rhyming pattern creates a powerful image.

ESSAY STYLE QUESTIONS

1. Compare and contrast the theme of reality vs. appearance in *The Taming of the Shrew.*

2. Using examples from **Act II Scene II**, and other examples from *Romeo and Juliet,* how does Shakespeare explore the relationship between Romeo and Juliet? Focus on language, imagery and themes.

3. How is Orlando's and Rosalind's relationship portrayed? Consider the use of language and imagery.

4. What contrasts are conveyed in *A Midsummer Night's Dream*? Why are they important?

ANSWERS TO UNDERSTANDING PLAYS

ROMEO AND JULIET

Q1.

The imagery conveyed in this passage is primarily religious. Both Romeo and Juliet use language which clearly makes reference to religion. This is established through the use of the words, *"holy shrine," "saints," "prayer"* and *"sin"*. The use of religious imagery in Shakespeare's language conveys the idea of purity, and how the characters of Romeo and Juliet are drawn to one another, just as pilgrims are drawn to the holy shrine. At the time, religion played a huge role in society, and therefore audiences would be able to relate to this.

Q2.

The first 14 lines of this passage (up until Romeo kisses Juliet) read as a sonnet. Between the two, they confess their attraction towards one another. This reinforces the main theme of *Romeo and Juliet,* which is love. The whole narrative is centred around the concept of love, and the first meeting between the two lovers conveys this; through the use of poetic conventions. Just like a sonnet, these 14 lines read with passion in mind. The use of rhythm allows the audience to feel a sense of romance. The structure follows an *ABAB* rhyme scheme. For example, *"If I profane with my unworthiest hand / This holy shrine, the gentle sin is this: / My lips, two blushing pilgrims, ready stand / To smooth that rough touch with a tender kiss."* This shows how Shakespeare uses poetic techniques in order to emphasise themes such as love and passion.

Q3.

The phrase *"My unworthiest hand"* implies that Romeo does not deem himself as being a worthy suitor for Juliet. The fact that his hand is unworthy also relates to the conflict between his family (the Montagues) and her family (the Capulets).

Q4.

Shakespeare suggests that the sin which Romeo has committed by touching Juliet's hand needs to be erased, and so he wishes to make this up with a kiss. However, after their kiss, Juliet informs him that she is now in possession of his sin, and that he must kiss her again so she is free from the sin.

THE TAMING OF THE SHREW

Q1.

Petruchio repeats Kate's name several times. The fact that he repeats her name is emphasising how he is in control of her. He uses her name as a way of showing Katherina that he holds power and dominance. Addressing her directly shows his affection, however although this could be seen as undermining and child-like.

Q2.

Petruchio's attempt to woo Katherina suggests that he is trying to counteract everything she says in order to assert his authority. For example, Petruchio claims the following: *"Say that she frown, I'll say she looks as clear as morning roses newly wash'd with dew. Say she be mute and will not speak a word, then I'll commend her volubility and say she uttereth piercing eloquence"*. This reinforces how he will antagonise her, hoping that she falls for his determination and willingness to stick by her.

Q3.

Petruchio repeats her name by addressing her as "Kate", even after she states that everyone should address her as Katherina. Again, this shows his attempts to antagonise her, and his affection for her.

Q4.

There is a clear power struggle in the relationship between Katherina and Petruchio. Katherina is shown to be an independent woman, who says what she thinks. She refuses to be dominated by male figures. The fact that Petruchio attempts to dominate her, shows that he has control over her. In modern society, the saying that 'opposites attract' could be applied to their relationship; the fact that they are completely opposite to one another suggests that they are a perfect match.

AS YOU LIKE IT

Q1.

The sentence *"I rather will subject me to the malice of a diverted blood and bloody brother,"* suggests that the relationship between Orlando and Oliver is quite hostile. The fact that Oliver is trying to get rid of Orlando by killing him is reinforced through the use of the word *"blood."* Orlando states that he would rather give himself up to his violent brother, as opposed to running away.

Q2.

Shakespeare's language *"when service sweat for duty, not for meed"* reinforces how people used to work because it was their duty, as opposed to simply working for money. This is completely different to modern day society. In modern times, people work to provide for themselves and their families, whereas years ago people worked for pleasure and obligation.

Q3.

The relationship between Orlando and Adam is amicable. Adam is older than Orlando and has good intentions to try and protect Orlando from his brother. He offers his savings for Orlando to start over somewhere new. The fact that Adam states *"let me be your servant. Though I look old, yet I am strong and lusty"* reinforces how Adam attempts to provide help to his friend. He also states that he will work for his *"master"*. This shows a close relationship. We can see that it's not just based on a servant and master working relationship, but that they are also friends.

Q4.

In Adam's speech, beginning with *"Master, go on, and I will follow thee,"* Shakespeare uses rhyming couplets. Shakespeare uses these rhyming couplets as a way of emphasising the noble and decent characteristics of Adam. Although he is a servant, the fact that Shakespeare has chosen to use a rhyming pattern for this character suggests that he is deemed important and righteous. This creates a powerful image for the audience, by providing lower class citizens with characteristics that are often conveyed in higher class people.

ESSAY STYLE QUESTIONS

1. *Compare and contrast the theme of reality vs. appearance in The Taming of the Shrew.*

- There are many occurrences of where reality versus appearance is apparent in *The Taming of the Shrew.*

- Within this play, we see physical disguises of certain characters, deceptive and psychological changes in behaviour, and changes in attitude and actions.

- For example:

  o   Lucentio disguised as a tutor, in hope to woo Bianca.

  o   Tranio disguised as his master (Lucentio).

  o   Hortensio disguised as a tutor, in hope to woo Bianca.

  o   Katherina's transition from a shrew to a tamed wife.

  o   Bianca's ability to appear sweet and innocent, but also has characteristics similar to her sister.

- Another example of appearance that plays a crucial element in the relationship between Katherina and Petruchio, is Petruchio's wedding costume. His old-fashioned clothing was worn to embarrass Katherina and make the point that he is in control.

- Bianca appears to be a goody-two-shoes who is only interested in her education. Yet, her private tutoring lessons see Bianca flirt with male suitors.

QUOTATIONS TO CONSIDER:

"And place your hands below your husband's foot"

- This reinforces how Katherina is conveyed as being tamed at the end of the play. Is this accurate? Or do you think Katherina is putting on an appearance?

Stage direction – *Enter Tranio disguised as Lucentio and the Merchant, booted and bare headed, dressed like Vincentio.*

- This shows how characters are appearing to be people that they are not.

This is a visual depiction of the theme reality vs. appearance.

"And yet I come not well"

- This quote signifies how Petruchio has come dressed poorly to his wedding to Katherina. This emphasises how his appearance suggests how he wants to humiliate Katherina. The reality is, Katherina has to marry him because nobody else wants to marry a 'shrew'.

"Fie, what a foolish duty call you this?"

- Bianca also carries characteristics as being a shrew, just like her sister. She tries to resist being controlled by a male figure (Lucentio).

2. *Using examples from **Act II Scene II**, and other examples from Romeo and Juliet, how does Shakespeare explore the relationship between Romeo and Juliet? Focus on language, imagery and themes.*

- You can talk about this idea of coming-of-age romance.

- You can discuss how they are both willing to defy their parents and run away with one another – despite the family feuds between her family and his.

- Their love is conveyed in a strong, poetic way.

- Find different quotes and examples that use specific themes and imagery in order to convey this idea of romance.

- Romeo continues to express his love throughout the play.

- The pivotal scenes, the balcony scene and the death scene, highlight the strength of their love. The death scene in particular shows how they are willing to do anything (including killing themselves) in order to be with one another.

- You can talk about how Shakespeare explores this idea of classic romantic love.

QUOTATIONS TO CONSIDER:

"You kiss by th' book"

- This shows how Juliet teases Romeo for being very conventional in his ways of 'wooing' her.

"It is too rash, too unadvis'd, too sudden"

- Juliet realises how quickly their romance has escalated. Not only does this show naivety and innocence, but it also shows the strength of their love for one another.

"Did my heart love till now? Forswear it, sight! For I ne'er saw true beauty till this night."

- Romeo questions whether he's been in love before (with Rosalind), after seeing Juliet for the very first time.

"My lips, two blushing pilgrims, ready stand
To smooth that rough touch with a tender kiss"

- The language used in the dialogue between Romeo and Juliet is romantic, expressive, and poetic. This use of language clearly captures the romance between these two characters, which is probably why the play *Romeo and Juliet* can be classed as one of the all-time best love stories in literary history.

3. *How is Orlando's and Rosalind's relationship portrayed? Consider the use of language and imagery.*

- The relationship between Rosalind and Orlando is central to the topic of love.

- Rosalind falls in love after she watches Orlando wrestle with Charles. This shows how Rosalind falls in love with someone she hasn't got to know.

- The fact that Rosalind is disguised for the majority of the play as a man, whilst in pursuit of Orlando, suggests how their relationship began in an untraditional sense.

- Their love is articulated through the use of poetic language. This is emphasised by the carvings left for one another on trees in the forest.

- Rosalind and Orlando only meet a couple of times without the disguise of Ganymede. How then, could they possibly be in true love? You can discuss how the disguise of Rosalind makes their love questionable.

QUOTATIONS TO CONSIDER:

"The truest poetry is the most feigning"

- Touchstone describes the love of Rosalind and Orlando as being dishonest and misguided. Did they rush into their relationship? Were these two characters blindsided by one another? Is their love real or are they more fascinated with the idea of love rather than being in love?

"Men have died from time to time, and worms have eaten them, but not for love"

- Rosalind rejects Orlando's statement that he will die if she didn't love him in return. This shows the sheer magnitude of Orlando's feelings for Rosalind.

"O Rosalind! These trees shall be my books / And in their barks my thoughts I'll character"

- This is a visual depiction of how Orlando expresses his love for Rosalind by marking his words into the trees bark.

"Sir you have wrestled well, and overthrown / More than your enemies"

- Rosalind falls in love with Orlando at first sight. This is also shown by her giving him her necklace.

"My affection hath an unknown bottom"

- Again, this shows the strength of the love that Rosalind carries for Orlando.

4. *How does Shakespeare explore different contrasts in A Midsummer Night's Dream? Why are they important?*

- There are many contrasts that you can discuss for this question:
   o Magic versus normality
   o Dreams versus reality
   o Night versus day
   o Characters behaviour and appearance (Puck plays pranks on characters, whereas Bottom is the victim of the pranks)
   o Beauty versus ugly
   o Characters from Greek mythology, English folklore and classical literature

- Whatever contrasts you discuss in your answer, you need to support your answer by suggesting why Shakespeare has used these contrasts. What effect do they have on the audience and how does this tie in with the overall theme of the narrative?

- For example:

  o   The beauty of Titania, who weaves flowers in the hair of the ass-headed Bottom shows two visual juxtapositions.

  o   The fairies are represented as being graceful and magical, which contrasts with the characters of the craftsmen who are clumsy.

QUOTATIONS TO CONSIDER:

"I have had a most rare vision. I have had a dream, past the wit of man to say what dream it was"

- This contrasts the reality with this idea of dreams and visions.

"Base and vile" and "form and dignity"

- How qualities can be transformed.

"We cannot fight for love, as men may do"

- This shows the difference between men and women in terms of love. It show what women can and can't do in comparison to men.

UNDERSTANDING POETRY

UNDERSTANDING POETRY

WHAT IS POETRY?

Poetry is another form of literary writing.

Poems are often written to express feelings, thoughts or ideas. The subject of the poem will depend on what *type* of poem it is.

TYPES OF POETRY

Below is a list of the *types* of poems you will be expected to know for your assessments.

Sonnet

Lyrical
14 lines
10 syllables to a line
Often about love

Narrative

Tells a long story
Voice of narrator
or character
Do not have to rhyme

Tanka

Originate in Japan
5 lines
Syllable count of 5 / 7 / 5 / 7 / 7
Use of similes, metaphors or
personification

Limerick

5 lines
Lines 1, 2 and 5 rhyme
Lines 3 and 4 rhyme
To make you laugh

Cinquain

5 lines
'Cinq' = 5 in French
Syllable count of 2 / 4 / 6 / 8 / 2

Couplet

2 lines for a verse
Both lines rhyme

Haiku

Originate in Japan
3 lines
Syllable count of 5 / 7 / 5
Often about nature

Acrostic

Word written vertically
Each letter starts sentence
All lines should relate
to the topic of the poem

Ode

Ancient Greece
Lyric poem
Praise of a person or thing
Deep feelings or emotions

Free Verse

Follows no rules
Rhythm, syllables, number of lines,
topic = can be anything

UNDERSTANDING POETRY

GETTING TO GRIPS WITH POETRY TECHNIQUES

Not only is poetry a form of writing, but it's also a way for poets to express their feelings or ideas through the use of poetry techniques.

I have outlined below the key techniques to consider when creating poetry.

A stanza is a series of lines that forms paragraph-like blocks of text. Each stanza is separated with a line space.

The best way to identify a poem's stanza is to count the number of lines in each paragraph.

2 lines = couplet
3 lines = tercet
4 lines = quatrain
5 lines = cinquain
6 lines = sestet
7 lines = septet
8 lines = octave

The number of lines in a poem will depend on what type of poem it is. For example, a haiku poem will usually consist of 3 lines.

A poem will take a particular form. There are many different forms of poetry, and each of which will determine the rhythm, structure and content of the poem.

Lyrical – expressing strong emotions and feelings.

Narrative – telling a story through the use of characters, plotlines, and conversation.

Descriptive – describing the world through the use of elaborate images and adjectives.

UNDERSTANDING POETRY

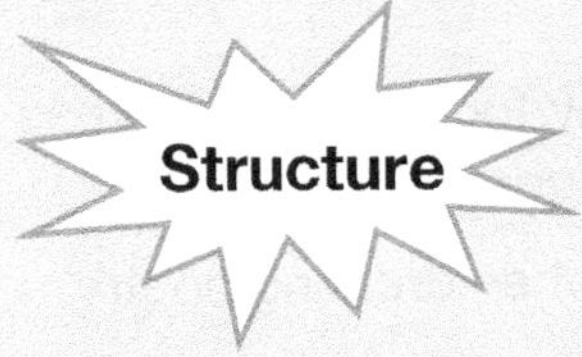

Structure

A poem's structure will depend on what type of poem it is.

Like a story, it has a structure. The story develops using a beginning, a middle and an end.

A poem will use a certain number of lines, verses, rhythms and rhymes to create a story.

<u>Below is a poem by Robert Louis Stevenson called 'Windy Nights'.</u>

Whenever the moon and stars are set,
Whenever the wind is high,
All night long in the dark and wet,
A man goes riding by.
Law in the night when the fires are out
Why does he gallop and gallop about?

Whenever the trees are crying aloud,
And ships are tossed at sea,
By, on the highway, low and loud,
By at the gallop goes he.
By at the gallop he goes, and then
By he comes back at the gallop again.

- Above shows two verses.
- There are 6 lines in each verse.
- The rhyming pattern for the verses is ABABCC.

Can you see how the poet uses different poetry conventions in order to tell the story?

The poet will often express their writing through the use of sound patterns.

Sound patterns are a great way for a reader to understand the rhythm and meaning behind the content of the poem.

➤ Rhyme

The repetition of similar sounding words. This is mostly done with the end words of sentences.

*Looking at the starry **night**,*

*The stars and moon that shone so **bright**.*

➤ Rhythm

Rhyme and rhythm are NOT the same thing. The rhythm of a poem is the beat you can hear as you read the poem.

The rhythm is created through 'stressed' and 'unstressed' words.

<u>Another way to create sound patterns is the emphasis on groups of words:</u>

➤ Alliteration

Alliteration is the repetition of repeating the same initial in the same line.

*Small **S**am **s**wam **s**lowly.*

Large, loud lion.

➤ Onomatopoeia

These are words that are used that sound like what they are describing.

'bang'   *'quack'*   *'moo'*   *'crash'*   *'pow'*

➤ Repetition

The use of repeating a word or phrase. This is done in order to emphasise key themes or ideas.

UNDERSTANDING POETRY

One of the biggest things to remember when writing or analysing poetry is the use of language.

Poets will use specific language in order to create meaning.

FIGURATIVE LANGUAGE

Figurative language involves using "figures of speech" that are used to create more of an impact and effect on its reader.

This type of language does NOT have a literal meaning. Instead, it is used to describe someone or something in a way that goes beyond the intended meaning.

There are many ways in which figurative language can be conveyed.

➢ **Similes**

A simile is a figure of speech which compares one thing to another. The reason for this is to make the image more vivid and descriptive.

Most similes use the words "like" or "as".

As busy as a bee.

As cold as ice.

See how the above examples are describing something by comparing it to something else?

➢ **Metaphors**

Metaphors are another figure of speech which uses a word or phrase to describe an object or action, which is not literally appropriate.

Her bedroom is a zoo.

Time is money.

See how the bedroom is being described as a zoo. This could imply that her room is messy. Time is NOT actually money, but this is a way of saying that that you need to put the time in if you wish to make money – time is as valuable as money.

UNDERSTANDING POETRY

➤ Personification

Personification uses human characteristics to describe inanimate objects – giving objects or 'things' feelings or emotions, or human attributes.

The skies wept.

The flowers were begging for water.

The fact that the skies are weeping, suggests that it is raining.

The flowers were NOT literally begging for water, but this shows how much they needed it.

➤ Hyperbole

Hyperboles are exaggerated statements which make something seem more excessive than it actually is.

Your bags weigh a ton!

I am dying of laughter.

These above examples are statements that show exaggeration. The bag doesn't really weigh a literal ton, but is extremely heavy.

The person is not actually dying, but they have been laughing a lot.

➤ Irony

Irony is a way of using words or phrases in which the intent of those words actually carries the opposite meaning.

Irony does not always have to be taken negatively. Some poets often use a form of irony that allows the reader to overlook the meaning, and understand different attitudes or conflicting interpretations.

"Oh great! Now you've ruined it!"

You slip on a banana peel, after laughing at someone who slipped on ice.

In the first example, the person doesn't actually mean "great". He is using it to be ironic – he is using it to actually mean the opposite.

In the second example, it is ironic to slip on a banana peel after laughing at someone else who slipped first.

UNDERSTANDING POETRY

SHAKESPEARE AND HIS POEMS

Aside from his literary genius in creating plays, William Shakespeare also spent a great deal of his writing career producing poems.

In total, Shakespeare wrote 154 sonnets, and five long narrative poems. His long narrative poems are less well-known, and he is mostly famous for his exceptional play writing skills and love poems.

LONG NARRATIVE POEMS

Shakespeare wrote five long narrative poems, each with a particular theme or subject topic in mind. These were written during different times throughout his writing career.

- *A Lover's Complaint*
- *Venus and Adonis*
- *The Rape of Lucrece*
- *The Phoenix and the Turtle*
- *The Passionate Pilgrim*

SONNETS

Shakespeare wrote 154 sonnets, each numbered (1-154).

Traditionally, a sonnet is a 14 line poem which is written in iambic pentameter. Shakespeare almost always used iambic pentameter when writing his sonnets.

<u>What is Iambic Pentameter?</u>

- Ten syllables to each line
- Five pairs of unstressed and stressed syllables (alternating)

(Da dum / da dum, / da dum, / da dum, / da dum)

Sometimes Shakespeare would break free from this, in order to add extra colour and feeling to his dialogue.

UNDERSTANDING POETRY

RHYMING PATTERNS

The rhyming pattern of English sonnets is as follows:

a b a b ⟶ Lines 1 and 3 rhyme / lines 2 and 4 rhyme

c d c d ⟶ Lines 5 and 7 rhyme / lines 6 and 8 rhyme

e f e f ⟶ Lines 9 and 11 rhyme / lines 10 and 12 rhyme

g g ⟶ Lines 13 and 14 rhyme

I have provided an example using Shakespeare's Sonnet 29, to emphasise the rhyming pattern:

SONNET 29

When in disgrace with Fortune and men's <u>eyes</u>,	**A**
I all alone beweep my outcast <u>state</u>,	**B**
And trouble deaf heaven with my bootless <u>cries</u>,	**A**
And look upon myself and curse my <u>fate</u>,	**B**
Wishing me like to one more rich in <u>hope</u>,	**C**
Featured like him, like him with friends <u>possessed</u>,	**D**
Desiring this man's art and that man's <u>scope</u>,	**C**
With what I most enjoy contented <u>least</u>,	**D**
Yet in these thoughts my self almost <u>despising</u>,	**E**
Haply I think on thee, and then my <u>state</u>,	**F**
(Like to the lark at break of day <u>arising</u>	**E**
From sullen earth) sings hymns at heaven's <u>gate</u>,	**F**
For thy sweet love remembered such wealth <u>brings</u>,	**G**
That then I scorn to change my state with <u>kings</u>.	**G**

Rhythm is a key technique used in poetry, in order to create emotions, mood and atmosphere.

Sonnets in particular use a beat to keep the momentum and flow of the narrative. For example, poems about love would have an upbeat, positive rhythm, whereas something more serious would have a very different beat.

UNDERSTANDING POETRY

ANALYSING SONNETS

The first 126 sonnets in Shakespeare's collection appear to address a man. These sonnets deal with themes including love, nobility, music, time and betrayal.

Sonnets 127 to 152 appear to address a woman. The themes in language in these poems seem much more personal and intense compared to the first 126 sonnets.

The last two sonnets seem trivial. They appear to be written in a similar style to that of Greek epigrams. Although these poems do touch upon the relationship between Shakespeare and the woman (in sonnets 127 to 152), these two poems take a different turn in terms of language and narration.

<u>When analysing sonnets, you should consider the following things:</u>

- Narration
- Tone of voice
- 1st person or 3rd person
- Imagery
- Themes
- Rhythm
- Mood
- Feelings
- Structure
- Context

POETRY TECHNIQUES IN HIS PLAYS

Shakespeare often used poetic devices in his plays. He did this on purpose and it proved really effective in theatre performances.

Most of Shakespeare's plays were written using iambic pentameter. He used this technique for the dialogue of higher-class characters. For lower-class characters, they would speak in prose as opposed to verses.

This would differentiate the social standings between different characters.

The Raven by Edgar Allan Poe

Once upon a midnight dreary, while I pondered, weak and weary,
Over many a quaint and curious volume of forgotten lore –
While I nodded, nearly napping, suddenly there came a tapping,
As of some one gently rapping, rapping at my chamber door.
"'Tis some visitor," I muttered, "tapping at my chamber door –
Only this and nothing more."

Ah, distinctly I remember it was in the bleak December;
And each separate dying ember wrought its ghost upon the floor.
Eagerly I wished the morrow; - vainly I had sought to borrow
From my books surcease of sorrow – sorrow for the lost Lenore –
For the rare and radiant maiden whom the angels name Lenore –
Nameless *here* for evermore.

And the silken, sad, uncertain rustling of each purple curtain
Thrilled me – filled me with fantastic terrors never felt before;
So that now, to still the beating of my heart, I stood repeating
"'Tis some visitor entreating entrance at my chamber door –
Some late visitor entreating entrance at my chamber door; –
That it is and nothing more."

Presently my soul grew stronger; hesitating then no longer,
"Sir," said I, "or Madam, truly your forgiveness I implore;
But the fact is I was napping, and so gently you came rapping,
And so faintly you came tapping, tapping at my chamber door,
That I scarce was sure I heard you" – here I opened wide the door; –
Darkness there and nothing more.

QUESTION 1

Poe's *'The Raven'* is an example of a narrative style poem. From the first line of the poem, how can you tell that the atmosphere of this narrative is going to be melancholic and sad?

QUESTION 2

Describe the rhyming pattern of the poem. What impact does this have on the reader?

QUESTION 3

Poe intentionally stresses the letter 'O' in his writing, particularly in the words of 'Lenore' and 'nevermore'. Why do you think the poet chooses this particular letter to stress? How does this tie in with the overall theme of the narrative?

QUESTION 4

Why do you think the fourth and fifth line ends with the same word?

QUESTION 5

What literary techniques can you point out within the four verses of *'The Raven'*?

QUESTION 6

How does this poem make you feel?

POEM 1

There once was a turtle named Joe,
Considered the slowest of the slow.
He entered the race,
With slow as his pace,
On your marks, get set, go!

POEM 2

There once was a giant so smelly,
Proud of his overgrown belly.
Feared by all,
Except his friend Paul,
Who told him to cut down on jelly.

POEM 3

There was a boy who loved French bread,
Whose dear mother had often said:
'Cut down or you'll bloat,
Like an oversized goat,
You'll never get out of bed'.

POEM 4

There once was a group of old ladies,
Who roamed around in their Mercedes.
Cheeky as chimps,
With staggering limps,
Following the rules of ol' Hades.

QUESTION 1

What type of poems are poems 1, 2, 3 and 4? Circle **one.**

| Haiku | Tanka | Limerick | Sonnet |

QUESTION 2

Give a definition of the poem you have circled.

____

____

QUESTION 3

Which words in Poem 3 are used to rhyme with "bread"?

_______________________ and _______________________

QUESTION 4

Describe how all four of these poems have a similar rhythmic structure. Compare at least **two** poems.

____

____

____

____

____

____

____

____

____

QUESTION 5

Using the language and structure of poems 1 to 4, do you think you could use this structure to write about something more serious or sad? Tick **yes** or **no**.

YES   **NO**

Explain your answer.

____

____

____

____

____

____

QUESTION 6

There are two similes used in the poems above, rewrite the simile, and state which poem it is from, and why the poet has used that simile.

Simile 1

Poem = _______________________

Simile = ____

Why is it used? = _________________________________

____

Simile 2

Poem = _______________________

Simile = ____

Why is it used? = _________________________________

____

Sonnet 1 by William Shakespeare

From fairest creatures we desire increase,
That thereby beauty's rose might never die,
But as the riper should by time decrease,
His tender heir might bear his memory:
But thou contracted to thine own bright eyes,
Feed'st thy light's flame with self-substantial fuel,
Making a famine where abundance lies,
Thyself thy foe, to thy sweet self too cruel.
Thou that art now the world's fresh ornament,
And only herald to the gaudy spring,
Within thine own bud buriest thy content,
And, tender churl, mak'st waste in niggarding.
Pity the world, or else this glutton be,
To eat the world's due, by the grave and thee.

QUESTION 1

Shakespeare explores this idea of beauty and nature. Find two quotes from the sonnet to demonstrate his ideas.

1. ____

2. ____

QUESTION 2

What do the words *"rose"* and *"bud"* imply in this sonnet? What connotations are created?

____

____

____

____

____

____

____

____

____

____

____

____

QUESTION 3

Explain how Shakespeare explores the idea of time, using examples from the passage.

QUESTION 4

What does line 2 in the sonnet mean? What theme is being conveyed?

QUESTION 5

"From fairest creatures we desire increase"

The use of the word *"increase"* could convey two possible meanings. The increase could be referring to commercial gain (i.e. money).

What other possible theme could the term "increase" suggest? Use another example from the sonnet to support your answer.

Have I Told You Lately? by How2Become

Have I told you lately that you are my world?
My feelings inside all spiralled and swirled.
A love so precious, a love so true,
A love I send from me to you.

Have I told you lately that you are my best friend?
Our lives together, beautifully transcend.
A love so honest, a love so pure,
A love I cherish for evermore.

Have I told you lately you complete my heart?
We are so strong, we'll never part.
A love so tender, a love so real,
A love that I will always feel.

Have I told you lately that you are everything?
A relationship as beautiful as a butterfly wing.
A love for always, a love forever,
I love you, forever and ever.

QUESTION 1

Describe the structure and rhythm of *'Have I Told You Lately?'*

QUESTION 2

Why do you think the author has begun every verse with the words 'Have I told you lately...'?

QUESTION 3

Why do you think the last line of the poem differs from the other last lines of each verse?

QUESTION 4

The author uses a simile in the poem. Write the simile and explain how this fits in with the narrative of the poem.

QUESTION 5

Why do you think this poem is written in 1st person?

QUESTION 6

Write a verse for this poem which uses the same structure and rhyming pattern. Explain how your verse ties in with the theme of the poem, and what you considered when writing your verse.

ANSWERS TO UNDERSTANDING POETRY

THE RAVEN

Q1.

From the first line, "once upon a midnight dreary", we can tell that this poem is going to be melancholic and sad. Unlike stories beginning with 'once upon a time' Poe's choice of words suggests the exact opposite from a story of a fairy tale. The use of the words "midnight" and "dreary" imply that Poe's feelings are much more pessimistic and gloomy.

Q2.

The rhyming pattern of the poem is as follows: the second, fourth, fifth and sixth line rhyme. The rhyming pattern is ABCBBB. This creates a rhythmic beat for the reader and makes it compelling to read. The fact that the tone of the poem is quite down beaten, makes the rhythm that much more eerie and sad.

Q3.

The use of the letter 'O', particularly in the words of "Lenore" and "nevermore" suggests an eerie tone. If you think of the words 'O', it elongates to sound spooky. This helps to create the pessimistic tone that Poe was intentionally trying to create.

Q4.

The fourth and fifth line ends with the same word as it allows the reader to understand the important words that Poe was trying to highlight. As we can see, Poe repeats the words "door" and "Lenore". These two words must play a significant part in the rest of the poem's narrative.

Q5.

Literary techniques that you could talk about include:

- Alliteration = 'silken, sad'   'entreating entrance'   'lost Lenore'
- Onomatopoeia = 'tapping'   'rustling'

Q6.

This response requires your personal feelings. How does the poem make YOU feel? Why do you think the poet chooses to create these feelings within the narrative of this poem?

POEMS 1 – 4

Q1.

Limerick.

Q2.

A limerick is a poem that uses rhythm and rhyming patterns with the intention to be funny and/or silly.

Q3.

'Said' and 'bed'.

Q4.

All of the poems follow the same rhythmic structure. The last word of the first, second and last line rhyme. The third and fourth line rhyme. For example, in Poem 1, lines 1, 2 and 5 end with the words "Joe", "slow" and "go". Lines 3 and 4 end with the words "race" and "pace". In Poem 3, lines 1, 2 and 5 end with the words "bread", "said" and "bed". Lines 3 and 4 end with the words "bloat" and "gloat".

Q5.

This answer is based on personal preference, you just need to provide solid reasoning for your choice.

<u>For example:</u>

You could circle "no" because the structure and style of these poems are upbeat, funny and silly. The tone of these poems is very laid back and therefore could not be used to talk about something more serious.

Q6.

- *"Like an oversized goat" (poem 3).*

The poet has used this simile not only for humorous effect, but also to emphasise that the boy's overeating mirrors an engorged animal.

- *"Cheeky as chimps" (poem 4).*

The poet uses this simile to suggest that the old ladies are lively, immature and bold – the same characteristics as a chimp.

SONNET 1

Q1.

"That thereby beauty's rose might never die"

"And only herald to the gaudy spring"

Q2.

The words "rose" and "bud" suggest the idea of blossoming. This could be in relation to age, or it could suggest the blossoming of love, and how it is growing.

Q3.

The sonnet explores this idea of human life and time. Shakespeare explores this idea of procreating and continuing legacy through children. The line "but as the riper should by time decrease" is talking about when a parent dies and how the "heir" (their child) will continue those memories.

Q4.

Line two, "that thereby beauty's rose might never die" suggests immortality. If the beauty of a person does not die, it continues to live – through the use of a child.

Q5.

The word "increase" could be talking about an offspring i.e. procreating. The sonnet does draw upon this idea through the line "his tender heir might bear his memory". The use of the words "increase" and "heir" imply similar connotations.

HAVE I TOLD YOU LATELY?

Q1.

The structure of this poem consists of four verses, each with 4 lines. Each verse contains the rhyming pattern of AABB. For example, in the first verse, line 1 and line 2 rhyme with 'world' and 'swirled', and line 3 and line 4 rhyme with 'true' and 'you'.

Q2.

The writer uses a rhetorical question to begin each verse in order to immediately make it personal to whoever is reading the poem. A rhetorical question is a literary technique which writers can use when the question does not actually require an answer. The writer is answering their own question. This makes the poem read effectively and makes it more descriptive.

Q3.

The last line of the poem differs from the other last lines of each verse because it is summing up the entirety of the poem. It makes it clear that the writer is in love, and the last line 'I love you, forever and ever' not only makes it memorable, but it also has a timeless connotation.

Q4.

The simile in the poem is "a relationship as beautiful as a butterfly wing". This simile is great as it is comparing a relationship with the beauty, nature and freedom that can be found in a butterfly.

Q5.

The poem is written in 1st person in order to make the poem more personal. Not only that, but the reader is also reading the poem as a personal account of the writer. It looks as though the writer has put themselves at the heart of the story.

Q6.

This answer requires you to come up with your own verse for this poem, which uses the same structure and rhyming pattern. Make sure your verse ties in with the overall themes of the poem.

Have someone read your verse and see what they think. What do they like about your verse? What didn't they like? How could you improve?

This question is great because it not only assesses how well you understand what you've read, but how well you can put that thought-process into creative writing.

HOW ARE YOU GETTING ON?

NEED A LITTLE EXTRA HELP WITH KEY STAGE THREE (KS3) ENGLISH?

How2Become have created these other FANTASTIC guides to help you and your child prepare for their Key Stage Three (KS3) English assessments.

FOR MORE INFORMATION ON OUR KEY STAGE 3 (KS3) GUIDES, PLEASE CHECK OUT THE FOLLOWING:

WWW.HOW2BECOME.COM

Get Access To

FREE

Psychometric Tests

www.PsychometricTestsOnline.co.uk

Printed and bound by CPI Group (UK) Ltd, Croydon, CR0 4YY

25/03/2025

01836314-0002